REYNARD THE FOX

Adapted from *Gestes de Renart le Goupil*

by

ARTHUR FAUQUEZ

Translation by Marie-Louise Roelants

With Costume-Make-Up Designs by
IRENE COREY

Introduction by
MOUZON LAW

ANCHORAGE PRESS, INCORPORATED
Post Office Box 8067
NEW ORLEANS, LOUISIANA 70182

ROYALTY NOTE

The possession of this book, without a written authorization first having been obtained from the publisher, confers no right or license to professionals or amateurs, to produce the play publicly or in private, for gain or charity.

In its present form this play is dedicated to the reading public only, and not to producers. However, productions of this play are encouraged, and those who wish to present it may secure the necessary permission by writing to Anchorage Press, Incorporated, Post Office Box 8067, New Orleans, Louisiana 70182.

This play may be presented by amateurs upon payment to the Anchorage Press of a royalty of $25.00 for each performance, one week before the date of the play's opening. This play is fully protected by copyright, and anyone presenting it without the consent of the Anchorage Press will be liable to the penalties provided by the copyright law.

Professional producers are requested to apply to the Anchorage Press for royalty quotation.

Whenever the play is produced, the name of the author must be carried in all publicity, advertising, fliers, and programs. Also the following notice must appear on all printed programs: "Produced by special arrangement with The Anchorage Press, of New Orleans, Louisiana."

Reynard the Fox was first produced, under the title of "Le Roman de Renart", in 1958, by the Theatre de l'Enfance in Brussels, Belgium, under the direction of Jose Geal, and was subsequently toured across Belgium, in more than a hundred performances.

Translated from the French by Marie-Louise Roelants, an abridged version was presented in 1960 by the Madison, Wisconsin Theatre Guild, under the direction of Donald Von Buskirk.

The first full American premiere was presented in 1961 by the Department of Drama of the University of Texas, at Austin, Texas, under the direction of Mouzon Law. For this occasion, the costumes were designed by Lucy Barton, the set created by H. Neil Whiting.

A subsequent production of *Reynard the Fox* was presented in 1962 by the Jongleurs of Centenary College, at Shreveport, Louisiana, under the direction of Orlin Corey. This was the first production to make use of the animal costume-make-up designs provided for the play by Irene Corey.

INTRODUCTION

In the domain of current dramatic literature for children, REYNARD THE FOX stands apart — very much as Reynard, himself, stands apart from his *confrères* in the animal kingdom. Both the character, and the play about him, are unconventional in the context of their societies. This unconventionality — this individuality — is the strength of both.

Reynard's subtle charm, his wise way, his lack of pretention, his unalloyed honesty about himself, his *joie de vivre* tempered with his realistic approach to life, his bright, brave, good natured wit, render him without peer in his society and place his services in demand. By the same token, the unusual qualities of the script render it a departure from most plays for children and point to a possible new direction in children's theatre which may place the services of mature artists in greater demand for child audiences.

REYNARD THE FOX fulfills the necessary requirements of a script for children in that it tells an entertaining story, filled with colourful characters and their comic actions, with dramatic suspense. But . . . it goes further — much further:

Its theme wittily comments upon the good and the bad in everyone, and the hypocrisy of those who would be the judge of others.

Its characterizations of the animals are as subtle and as complex as are real people.

Its language is elevated. All of its story is not illustrated in action; some of it relies upon language alone for its communication — and that language oftentimes utilizes a vocabulary which extends the child's own.

Its type is essentially satire. It places on stage as the leading character with whom you are to sympathize, a rascal whose motives even in his heroic moments, are (realistically enough) tinged with a consideration of self. This fox is a satirical character, and the basic truth buried in his actions is inescapably satirical.

It plays on many levels of meanings, and its significance lies in its comment on the human counterparts of its animal characters.

REYNARD THE FOX asks the producing company to play to children, rather than play-down-to them. It asks children to understand a concept of human behaviour which may be at variance with the philosophical diet upon which they have fed.

In so doing, the play respects the intellect and the sensitivity of the child. In so doing, it also provides thought-provoking entertainment for the adult and, for that reason, has caused many an adult to question whether or not it is a play for children. In its pre-publication run, it caused not one child to question its suitability for them. They understood Reynard and were glad he was alive — and they went out of the theatre with something more than they had when they came in.

—MOUZON LAW

REYNARD THE FOX

by
Arthur Fauquez

Translation by Marie-Louise Roelants

CHARACTERS

Tiecelin, *the Crow*
Reverend Epinard, *the Hedgehog*
Brun, *the Bear*
Ysengrin, *the Wolf*
Noble, *the Lion*
Reynard, *the Fox*
Lendore, *the Marmot*

SYNOPSIS

The entire play takes place in the heart of the forest.

Prologue
    Scene 1. Spring
    Scene 2. Summer
    Scene 3. Autumn
    Scene 4. Winter
Epilogue

REYNARD THE FOX

by
Arthur Fauquez

PROLOGUE

(Tiecelin, perched in the crotch of a tree, practicing.)

TIECELIN: Caw! *(Higher)* Caw! *(Higher)* Caw!

(Brun enters, patch over one eye, his arm in a sling.)

BRUN: Stop that infernal racket!

TIECELIN: Caw! *(Higher)* Caw!

BRUN: Stop!

TIECELIN: You are interrupting my practice, Seigneur Brun. Caw!

BRUN: Stop this instant, and summon the King!

TIECELIN: *(notices him.)* The King? Good heavens, what has happened to you? Have you been caught in a bramble bush? Ha, ha, ha!

BRUN: Enough of your insolence! Call the King at once!

TIECELIN: Lord Bear, I am the King's Registrar. If you wish an audience with the King, you must state your reason to me.

BRUN: I have been beaten, do you hear? Look at me!

TIECELIN: Ha, ha, ha!

BRUN: I have been beaten, and it is all the fault of Reynard the Fox!

TIECELIN: Reynard did this to the mighty Bear?

BRUN: He tricked me. I want the King to punish him.

TIECELIN: Oh, if it was only one of Reynard's tricks —

BRUN: But look at me!

TIECELIN: I am. Ha, ha, ha!

(Ysengrin limps in, on a crutch, his head bandaged.)

YSENGRIN: Sound the trumpets!

TIECELIN: Baron Ysengrin!

BRUN: You, too?

TIECELIN: What a pair! Ha, ha, ha!

YSENGRIN: One more caw from you, Crow, and I'll wring your scrawny neck. Summon the King!

TIECELIN: The King is not to be called just because you stubbed your toe.

YSENGRIN: Stubbed my toe? I have been attacked by dogs. Look at me!

TIECELIN: Yes, I see. Ha, ha, ha!

BRUN: Who has done this to you?

YSENGRIN: It is all the doing of Reynard the Fox!

BRUN: Gr-r-r-r!

TIECELIN: Reynard did this to the powerful Wolf?

YSENGRIN: He tricked me.

BRUN: Me, too.

BOTH: Summon the King!

TIECELIN: *(climbs down.)* Gentlemen, if I were to summon the King every time Reynard played a trick, he would soon appoint a new Registrar.

YSENGRIN: But this is not to be borne!

BRUN: I intend to accuse Reynard in court.

YSENGRIN: Yes. We'll bring him to trial.

BRUN: And we shall demand his punishment.

YSENGRIN: I shall demand his hanging.

TIECELIN: Hanging?

BRUN: Yes! We have had enough of his tricks.

YSENGRIN: We are going to get rid of the Fox!

TIECELIN: If you have been unable to get rid of him in the field, how do you expect to get rid of him in Court?

BRUN: The King will do us justice.

YSENGRIN: Bring us to the King!

TIECELIN: Gentlemen, I am a man of law, and I will give you my best legal advice. Go home and lick your wounds. Reynard will trick you in Court, just as he has tricked you in the field. You have no evidence.

BRUN: Evidence? What of my black eye? And my arm?

YSENGRIN: Look at my lame leg. And my head!

TIECELIN: Yes, ha, ha, ha! What a picture! Now you will excuse me. I must return to my practicing.

(He climbs up.)

BRUN: You miserable Crow! The King shall hear of your insolence!

YSENGRIN: If you had a little more meat on your bones, I should have a nice fat crow's wing for my supper!

TIECELIN: Caw!

BRUN: Save us from that deafening noise!

(Exit, holding his ears.)

TIECELIN: Caw!

YSENGRIN: Take care, Crow, that the Fox does not trick you.

(Exit, limping. Reynard enters, unseen by Tiecelin.)

TIECELIN: Ho, ho, ho! The Fox trick me? What a joke! I am too smart for that. Caw! Caw! Caw!

REYNARD: *(groaning with pain)* Oh-h-h-h-h!

TIECELIN: Can I never practice in peace? Caw-w-w-w — Good Heavens, it is the Fox himself!

REYNARD: *(weakly)* Tiecelin, my friend — Oh-h-h-h!

TIECELIN: What is your tale of woe? Do you wish to summon the King too?

REYNARD: No. I wish only to die in peace.

TIECELIN: To die?

REYNARD: Tiecelin, I have been poisoned.

TIECELIN: Poisoned?

REYNARD: Oh-h-h-h! It was an oyster I found. Sing me one of your sweetest songs, so that I may die with your music in my ears.

TIECELIN: You are not serious?

REYNARD: Sing, my good fellow

TIECELIN: Like this? Caw-w-w-w-!

REYNARD: Thanks, old friend.

(He gasps, then falls quiet.)

TIECELIN: Reynard? Reynard! Don't act the sleeping beauty. I know you. You are only faking. Oh, very well. I will rouse you. Caw! Caw! Caw! Not a wince. Not a quiver. He is very smart. Reynard? Is he really faking?

(He climbs down to look.)

My word, he sleeps like the dead. I can't even see him breathe. Good Heavens, he isn't breathing! Could he really be dead? What a release, Lord, if this is so!

(He moves Reynard's tail, which drops back, limp.)

But how could he be dead? This is too much to hope. He said an oyster. It is possible.

(He pokes the Fox with a long stick. Reynard rolls over, a dead weight.)

It's true! Brun! Ysengrin! No, I am the one who found him. It will win me the gratitude of the whole kingdom if I hint that I am a tiny bit responsible for this — oh, just a very tiny bit — just enough to make them think I am the one who liberated the world from this rascal. I should be hailed as a hero. I shall have my portrait painted in triumphant attire, crushing my vanquished enemy, and I shall sell his skin for a fur.

(He rests his foot upon Reynard, in a conqueror's pose.)

REYNARD: *(grasping his ankle)* Dear Tiecelin!

TIECELIN: Help! Help! He is not dead!

REYNARD: You had better learn, dear friend, never to sell Reynard's skin before you have killed him.

TIECELIN: What I said about it was only in fun. I — I only wanted to give you a laugh.

REYNARD: Well, you see, you succeeded. I am laughing. I am laughing with all my teeth, which in a few moments are going to gobble you up.

TIECELIN: You are not going to kill me like a simple chicken?

REYNARD: Why not?

TIECELIN: I am the Royal Registrar. And besides I am your friend.

REYNARD: Yes?

TIECELIN: Only a minute ago, I saved you from a Court trial.

REYNARD: I am very grateful, believe me. And because of that I'll swallow you in one gulp, without chewing.

TIECELIN: Let me go!

REYNARD: *(plucking a feather from Tiecelin's tail)* And moreover, I'll keep this to remember you by

TIECELIN: Aie! You have ruined my beautiful tail!

REYNARD: Never mind, Tiecelin. You will not be needing it any more.

TIECELIN: Oh-h-h, you monster! I am going to be eaten, and I can see no escape.

REYNARD: None whatever

TIECELIN: Then at least grant my last wish. If I have to be eaten, don't just gobble me down like a piece of cheese. Treat me as a delicacy, and prepare your stomach for this feast.

REYNARD: My stomach is always prepared.

TIECELIN: Oh, no. To enjoy a dainty morsel fully, it is necessary to warm your stomach and your head — like this.

(He rubs his stomach and his head.)

REYNARD: Why your head?

TIECELIN: To eat intelligently.

REYNARD: And why your stomach?

TIECELIN: To warm your appetite.

REYNARD: It is an odd method.

TIECELIN: But it works, I assure you.

REYNARD: Like this?

(*He lets go of Tiecelin, to rub head and stomach.*)

TIECELIN: Oh, harder than that.

REYNARD: It certainly does warm me up.

TIECELIN: (*clambering up to his perch*) The best way to digest well is to eat nothing.

REYNARD: Why, Tiecelin!

TIECELIN: You savage! Did you think I was going to let you eat me for lunch?

REYNARD: Eat you for lunch? I would have to be starving.

TIECELIN: I am going to denounce you to the King.

REYNARD: (*laughing*) Oh, Tiecelin, you take yourself so seriously.

TIECELIN: The King also will take me seriously. Trumpets!

(*Trumpets.*)

REYNARD: Caw! Caw! Caw! (*Mimicking*) Oh, Tiecelin, sing me one last song before I die.

(*Exit, laughing. Returns immediately.*)

By the way, keep this to remember me by.

(*Tosses feather. Exit.*)

TIECELIN: My feather! Monster! Thief! Cannibal!

(*He climbs down to retrieve the feather.*)

My beautiful feather! But this is evidence. Now we have him! Brun! Ysengrin! Bring the fox to trial! I have the evidence! Trumpets!

(*Trumpets. Epinard enters quietly.*)

EPINARD: My dear fellow, what are the trumpets all about?

TIECELIN: Reverend Epinard. Stand there. I am about to make a proclamation. Trumpets!

(*Trumpets.*)

We, Tiecelin the Crow, Royal Registrar, announce a great Court of Justice meeting, to put on trial the most infamous of all criminals, His Majesty's Own Knight —

(Drum roll.) Reynard the Fox!

EPINARD: Reynard, on trial? But will you explain —

TIECELIN: One moment. Whoever wishes to accuse the Fox is requested to give his name to the Registrar. I am the Registrar. Trumpets!

(Trumpets.)

EPINARD: What is this all about?

TIECELIN: It means, Reverend, that we are at last going to put Reynard on trial, and punish him for his misdeeds. Don't you yourself have some complaint to make against the Fox?

EPINARD: I?

TIECELIN: Yes, you. Has your religious robe protected you from his tricks?

EPINARD: Oh, no. Only last week, he got a duck-egg away from me.

TIECELIN: Well, then. You will lodge a charge against him?

EPINARD: Ahem! I should not wish it made public how I — ah — came by the duck-egg.

TIECELIN: As you wish. Sit over there. Here come two who will testify.

(Epinard sits and reads in his Bible. Brun and Ysengrin enter.)

YSENGRIN: You are bringing him to trial?

TIECELIN: I have the evidence.

BRUN: Where is the King?

(Noble the Lion enters, majestically, theatrically.)

NOBLE: Since when do the trumpets not greet my arrival?

TIECELIN: *(bowing)* Sire — your Majesty — I think — I thought — Trum — Trumpets!

(Trumpets.)

NOBLE: Let my arrival be announced to the Court.

TIECELIN: Yes, Sire. Trumpets!

(Trumpets.) Gentlemen, the King!

(All bow, as Noble seats himself.)

NOBLE: I declare the Court of Justice open. Now, Tiecelin, why have you assembled us all in Court?

TIECELIN: To hear charges against your Majesty's Knight, Sir Reynard the Fox.

NOBLE: Reynard? What charges?

YSENGRIN: I have been attacked!

BRUN: I have been beaten!

TIECELIN: My very life has been threatened!

NOBLE: Brun! Ysengrin! Where have you received these terrible injuries? Have you been fighting again?

BRUN: Sire, it is Reynard!

YSENGRIN: We are the victims of Reynard's trickery!

TIECELIN: This is Reynard's doing!

NOBLE: If this is true, Reynard is a dangerous criminal indeed. Bring him in.

TIECELIN: But your Majesty —

BRUN: We do not require his presence to recite his crimes.

YSENGRIN: We can tell you —

NOBLE: Where is Reynard?

TIECELIN: Knight Reynard thinks — he does not know — actually, I think he thinks —

NOBLE: Enough thinking. Where is Reynard?

TIECELIN: He th — I mean, he believes — your Majesty, I will have him brought before you.

NOBLE: Let this insolent character be called at once.

TIECELIN: Y-y-yes, Sire. S-s-s-sir Reynard the Fox! Trumpets!

(*Trumpets, resembling a hunter's call, ending with drum roll. During this fanfare, each animal makes his own preparations for Reynard's entrance, reflecting his attitude toward this dangerous criminal.*)

YSENGRIN: Here comes the villain!

(*Reynard enters, smiling, confident. Bows to the King.*)

NOBLE: I greet you, Knight Reynard.

REYNARD: Good evening, Sire.

NOBLE: Just answer our questions.

REYNARD: Allow me, Sire, to wish that this day may not go by without being the best one of your life.

NOBLE: Quiet. We have assembled the High Court of Justice, for the express purpose of putting you on trial.

REYNARD: On trial? Me? The most devoted and faithful of all your subjects? But why, Sire? What have I done to be tried for?

NOBLE: You shall know this very minute. Tiecelin, announce the first accuser.

TIECELIN: Master Ysengrin the Wolf.

NOBLE: We are listening, Ysengrin.

YSENGRIN: I accuse —

REYNARD: Cousin Ysengrin, you, my accuser?

YSENGRIN: I accuse! Do you deny that you led me into a farm-yard under the pretext of showing me a flock of nice, plump ducks?

REYNARD: Not at all. I did show you a flock of nice, plump ducks, Cousin. Is that a crime?

YSENGRIN: And do you deny that you fastened me in, and roused the dogs, so that I was so cruelly bitten, I barely escaped alive?

REYNARD: Oh, my dear Cousin, is that how you suffered those grievous wounds? Those dreadful dogs!

NOBLE: So you admit luring him into a trap where he almost lost his life?

REYNARD: Oh, no. Excuse me, Sire. I only took him to the farm-yard to show him nice, plump ducks, as he says. But when he saw them, he began to drool and slobber and lick his lips at the sight, and even started to chase them. I could not stay for this. I fled, and cried out for help. Was it my fault if the gate shut behind me, and locked Ysengrin in with the dogs?

NOBLE: If the story is as you tell it —

YSENGRIN: Allow me —

NOBLE: And I am inclined to believe you — the Marshal Ysengrin is as guilty as you are, and by the same token, deserves the same punishment. It is up to you, Lord Wolf, to fix Reynard's fate, since that fate shall be yours also. What punishment would you suggest?

YSENGRIN: Ah — uh — in that case — yes, in that case, I think it is better — and wiser — not to punish Reynard.

REYNARD: Thanks, dear Cousin, for your generous intervention.

NOBLE: This case is settled. Who is next, Tiecelin?

TIECELIN: Seigneur Brun.

NOBLE: It is your turn, Master Brun.

BRUN: I accuse!

REYNARD: You, my Uncle?

BRUN: Be quiet!

NOBLE: We are listening, Seigneur Brun.

BRUN: Your Majesty, I was taking a peaceful nap under an apple tree, when this creature —

REYNARD: Uncle.

BRUN: This mongrel —

REYNARD: Uncle.

BRUN: This rascal —

REYNARD: Uncle!

BRUN: For Heaven's sake, will you let me speak?

NOBLE: Proceed, Seigneur Brun.

BRUN: I was only sleeping, your Majesty, doing no harm to anyone —

REYNARD: He means, Sire, he was resting, after a large lunch. He had just stripped the apple tree, bare.

BRUN: It is not true! But this scoundrel found me there, and screamed for the farmer. Can you deny it?

REYNARD: No, not at all. I thought he was stricken, Sire. His belly was swollen till it looked like a barrel. I cried out in my grief. Could I help it if the farmer heard me? Uncle Brun heard me too, and tried to run away, but he was so full of apples, he couldn't even get to his feet.

BRUN: This is slander! He yelped for the farmer, your Majesty, and the farmer attacked me with a pitchfork. Before I could move from the spot, he gave me a black eye and four loose teeth, not to mention the hair and skin I lost in the fray.

NOBLE: If you had stolen his apples, Brun, it seems to me the punishment you received was justified. What do you think?

BRUN: I think — I think it was a very high price to pay for a few apples.

NOBLE: Forget it. Next one.

TIECELIN: The next one is myself: Master Tiecelin the Crow, Man of Law, and Royal Registrar.

NOBLE: What is your complaint against Reynard?

TIECELIN: I accuse!

REYNARD: Come, now.

TIECELIN: Yes! I accuse Reynard of trying, just a minute ago, to twist my neck and gobble me up, as simply as if I had been a chicken.

NOBLE: This is more serious. What have you to reply, Master Reynard?

REYNARD: One thing only. Look at this piteous carcass, and judge for yourself, Sire. Who would wish to gobble him up, skinny and emaciated as he is? And even if I did, am I any more guilty in this matter than my Cousin Ysengrin?

YSENGRIN: I protest!

REYNARD: Or my Uncle Brun?

BRUN: I deny it!

REYNARD: Or the cat, the dog, the sparrow, the vulture — or you yourself, Sire Lion, our very beloved King, as well?

(Laughter.)

NOBLE: Silence!

(Nobody laughs any more.)

Tiecelin, you over-estimate yourself. None of us wishes to eat crow.

TIECELIN: Reynard did. And here is the evidence. He pulled out one of my tail-feathers — this very feather.

REYNARD: Pouf! The wind plucks your feathers all the time.

TIECELIN: The wind!

(General laughter.)

NOBLE: Let's file this ridiculous case. Has anybody else any complaints against Reynard?

TIECELIN: Yes! The Reverend Epinard!

(He prods Epinard, who has appeared immersed in his Bible.)

EPINARD: Uh? Yes?

NOBLE: We are listening, Reverend Epinard.

EPINARD: You are listening to me? This doesn't happen every day.

(He opens his Bible, and prepares to preach.)

NOBLE: What charge do you wish to lodge against the red-haired Fox?

EPINARD: I?

TIECELIN: Remember — that duck-egg.

EPINARD: Duck-egg?

NOBLE: Look now, Reverend, has the Fox ever tried to harm you?

EPINARD: He wouldn't dare, Sire. My quills, you see.

NOBLE: If you have nothing to say, sit down. Is there any other accuser?

TIECELIN: Yes, Sire. There are countless ones. But they are not present.

NOBLE: Where are they?

TIECELIN: They are dead, Sire.

NOBLE: Dead?

TIECELIN: Yes, Sire. The rooster Chanticler, and his four hens. The drake, Halbran-des-Mares, and his three ducks. The guinea-fowl, Hupette. The turkey, Gloussard. And thousands of other winged creatures. All have met death and burial in the stomach of Reynard the Fox. Let's hang him, Sire.

YSENGRIN: Let's hang him upside down!

BRUN: Yes, he must hang!

NOBLE: That is a harsh judgement. Knight Reynard, can you think of any reason against it?

REYNARD: As many reasons as you have subjects, Sire. Doesn't my cousin Ysengrin himself devour innocent lambs and peaceful sheep? Doesn't my Uncle Brun treat himself to the honey he robs from the bees? Doesn't the Registrar Tiecelin eat the wheat and the grapes he steals from men? And you yourself, Sire, didn't you only yesterday have a gentle kid and half a deer for your supper?

YSENGRIN: We must hang him!

BRUN: Hang him!

TIECELIN: Hang him at once!

NOBLE: Do you hear?

REYNARD: I hear, Sire, and I don't worry too much, because I know there is more wisdom under a great King's crown than in the little brains of his courtiers. A very great King can forgive when need be.

NOBLE: A very great King can forgive when need be.

REYNARD: Mighty and gallant Majesty, I trust my fate to your hands.

NOBLE: I am a very great King, Reynard.

REYNARD: Without question, Sire.

NOBLE: You shall not hang.

REYNARD: Thank you, Sire.

TIECELIN: This is insane!

NOBLE: Who said that?

YSENGRIN: Sire, it is a mistake.

NOBLE: I pray you —

BRUN: If you will allow me, Sire —

NOBLE: I allow nothing! Silence, everybody, and let me render my sentence. You will not hang, Master Reynard. I grant you mercy for one more year.

TIECELIN: Mercy for one more year?

NOBLE: But this will be your last chance. In that year a record will be kept of your every crime.

BRUN: Of what use is a record, if he is left free to continue his crimes?

NOBLE: Twenty-four crimes we shall forgive you, without punishment.

YSENGRIN: Twenty-four crimes?

TIECELIN: Sire, this is proposterous!

NOBLE: Silence! We are all sinners, and hope for forgiveness. We shall forgive you twenty-four times.

REYNARD: You are a gracious King, Sire.

NOBLE: But take care. One crime more than twenty-four, and you shall be punished without mercy.

REYNARD: I understand, Sire.

NOBLE: One year from now, we shall hold court on this case again, and examine your record. Now you are free. Remember under what conditions.

REYNARD: Sire, you shall hear no further complaints from your humblest, most respectful servant, Reynard.

NOBLE: All right. Go.

REYNARD: I leave, Sire, broken-hearted to have earned the displeasure of so many esteemed friends.

(*Exit.*)

TIECELIN: Your Majesty, how can you —

YSENGRIN: Sire, this is madness!

BRUN: You have turned loose the greatest scoundrel in the kingdom!

TIECELIN: Who can keep track of all his crimes?

NOBLE: You will.

TIECELIN: I?

NOBLE: Yes. You are the Royal Registrar. I appoint you to keep a record book, and enter into it any crimes committed by Reynard.

TIECELIN: Thank you, your Majesty. It will give me pleasure.

NOBLE: I am very pleased with my judgement — stern, fair, but still merciful. Now, let each of you go peacefully back home, and recall my great justice.

TIECELIN: Trumpets!

(*Trumpets.*)

YSENGRIN: Hail to thee, Sire, Lion.

(*Aside*) What folly to let Reynard go free!

(*Exit.*)

BRUN: Hail, Sire.

(*Aside*) How foolish to forgive that redhair!

(*Exit.*)

NOBLE: You see, everybody is satisfied with my judgement. I am well satisfied myself. Good night, Tiecelin.

(Exit.)

TIECELIN: Good night, Sire.

(Aside) What a blunder, to leave that rascal at large!

(He goes to pinch Epinard's arm.)

EPINARD: Eh? Yes.

TIECELIN: It is all over, Reverend.

EPINARD: Yes, yes, I see. Moreover, it was very interesting. Very interesting indeed.

TIECELIN: I must say, you showed little interest in the cause of justice.

EPINARD: The cause of justice?

TIECELIN: Yes. Why didn't you tell the King about that duck-egg?

EPINARD: My dear fellow, I should not wish to earn Reynard's ill-will. The time might come when I should need Reynard on my side. Good night.

(Exit.)

TIECELIN: Good night, good night? How can I ever have another good night, after this? Reynard will make short work of me, if I give him the chance. My feathers rise with fear at the very thought.

(Lendore enters, half-asleep, pillow under her arm, bumps into Tiecelin, who freezes with terror.)

He has got me, already! Reynard?

LENDORE: What do you say?

TIECELIN: What? It is you? Lendore?

LENDORE: It's me.

TIECELIN: Why didn't you say something?

LENDORE: You didn't ask me anything.

TIECELIN: The Marmot. And I thought you were Reynard.

LENDORE: You didn't look at me very well.

TIECELIN: Where are you going?

LENDORE: To Reynard's trial. Is it here?

TIECELIN: The trial is over.

LENDORE: Already? I must have fallen asleep on my way.

TIECELIN: As usual.

LENDORE: How did it go?

TIECELIN: That rascal Reynard went scot-free, for a year!

LENDORE: Good!

TIECELIN: What is more, he is allowed to commit twenty-four crimes, without punishment.

LENDORE: Twenty-four? That will not take him long.

TIECELIN: But one crime more than twenty-four, and he shall hang! And I am appointed to keep the record.

LENDORE: The record?

TIECELIN: Yes. I am not the Royal Registrar for nothing. The King has appointed me to keep account of all his crimes. I shall make a book of them.

LENDORE: It is amazing how sleepy I still feel.

TIECELIN: Go to sleep, then. I intend to keep my eyes open, for the whole year.

LENDORE: *(settles to sleep, against a tree.)* Good night.

TIECELIN: It will be easy to accumulate twenty-five counts against him in a year. Ha, ha! I'll put an end to him, with my record-book.

End of Prologue

Scene One — Springtime

(Lendore enters, yawning. Reynard bounds in.)

REYNARD: Ah, Lendore! You have come out of your shelter. Spring is truly here.

LENDORE: Is it?

REYNARD: Melted is the cold snow that kept my feet wet all winter.

LENDORE: So it is.

REYNARD: Gone is the bitter frost that kept the burrows closed.

LENDORE: Ah, yes.

REYNARD: Quiet is the freezing wind that pinched my nose.

LENDORE: Excuse me. I don't hear any quiet.

REYNARD: Welcome, Spring — welcome to you, who brings back the innocent young rabbit, and the tender birdies, not to mention the dainty little chickens.

LENDORE: Go somewhere else to sing your Spring Song, Reynard. I need a nap.

(Sleeps. Ysengrin enters, quietly.)

REYNARD: *(at the overlook.)* Ah, look, Lendore. See the fine rooster in the farm-yard over there. I see you, Seigneur Coincoin. I have given you all winter to get fat, and now I am saving a place for you in my bag.

YSENGRIN: So! You are up to your old tricks, Reynard.

REYNARD: Cousin Ysengrin! You always tip-toe.

YSENGRIN: Naturally.

REYNARD: I was just — ah — admiring the spring.

YSENGRIN: You were just plotting to gobble up that rooster. I heard you.

REYNARD: I have always admired your ears, Ysengrin.

YSENGRIN: Just dare to attack that rooster. The King shall hear of it.

REYNARD: Very well, Cousin. I leave Seigneur Coincoin to you. Happy hunting!

(Exit.)

YSENGRIN: Happy hunting, indeed. That wily Fox would beat me to the farm-yard, if I let him.

(Lendore stirs.)

Ah! Perhaps I won't have to go so far as the farm-yard.

(Drooling, he quietly creeps up on her, with obvious intentions.

Reynard returns.)

REYNARD: Ah, Cousin, you have found what you want without hunting?

YSENGRIN: What brings you back here?

REYNARD: To do you a good turn, Cousin. I have found you a hunting companion. Here comes our Noble King.

(Noble enters, with zest and majesty.)

Your servant, Sire.

YSENGRIN: The Marmot, Sire. The Marmot. She sleeps.

NOBLE: Lendore, indeed. She has come out of her shelter. This is the herald of spring.

YSENGRIN: As you say, your Majesty.

NOBLE: Ysengrin, we have had to keep under cover all winter. Now I feel like hunting. Come and join me.

YSENGRIN: I am honoured, Sire. And — ah — Reynard?

NOBLE: Reynard has given up hunting for a year. Let's go.

(Exit.)

YSENGRIN: I am coming, Sire.

(To Reynard) You — you schemer!

(To Noble, off) I come!

(Exit.)

REYNARD: *(laughs.)* Happy hunting, Cousin.

(To Lendore) Lendore, Lendore, wake up.

LENDORE: Eh? What? What do you say?

REYNARD: Wake up. It is not wise to sleep when the hunting season is open.

LENDORE: I am a Marmot. It is the nature of a Marmot to sleep, any time.

REYNARD: Find yourself a private spot, then. And don't trust Ysengrin.

LENDORE: I don't trust anybody, Reynard — not even you.

REYNARD: Lendore.

LENDORE: All the same — I like you.

REYNARD: Thanks, old friend.

LENDORE: By the way, don't sit there. It is a bumble-bee nest.

(Exit.)

REYNARD: A bumble-bee nest? Fortunately she warns me. Ah, and here comes my Uncle Brun. What a heaven-sent opportunity to play a joke on him! But if the King should find out, there would be one of my twenty-four chances gone. Shall I do it? Yes! It is too good a chance to miss.

(Brun enters, out of sorts.)

Good morning, Uncle. Still grumbling?

BRUN: Leave me in peace.

REYNARD: That is just what I offer you. Let's make peace, and forget our little misunderstandings. As a token of good faith, I offer you some fair honey-cakes left by the bees. What do you think of that?

BRUN: I think it is another of your fabrications.

REYNARD: How unfortunate I am! My uncle himself doubts my sincerity.

BRUN: I don't believe a word. Where are those honey-cakes?

REYNARD: Why show them to you, since you don't believe there are any?

BRUN: And why, if they exist, don't you eat them yourself?

REYNARD: I am on probation for a year, Brun. It would count against me if I should rob the bees. Heigh-ho! Since you don't care for it, that honey will be lost to everyone.

(He makes a subtle move toward the bumble-bee nest.)

BRUN: *(to himself)* So there they are.

REYNARD: It's a shame.

BRUN: Yes. Too bad, isn't it? Well, I am off.

REYNARD: So am I. Good bye, Uncle.

BRUN: Good bye.

(Neither makes a move to go.)

Aren't you leaving?

REYNARD: Oh, certainly. And you?

BRUN: Me, too. So good bye.

(He pretends to leave.)

REYNARD: *(Pretending to leave also.)* Good bye.

BRUN: *(Comes back and finds himself in front of Reynard.)* I have lost something.

REYNARD: Can I help you look for it?

BRUN: Stupid of me. I left it at home. Good bye.

(Exit.)

REYNARD: Good bye, Uncle.

(Exit, but hides himself. Brun comes back.)

BRUN: *(Rushes to bumble-bee nest.)* Honey! That fool thought I was going to leave honey here to spoil!

(He puts his paw in the nest, withdraws it quickly.)

Bumble bees! The traitor!

(Bumble-bees come out in swarms and pursue him. Music. The flight of the bumble-bees can be suggested by light spots.)

Ah! Go away! My nose! Leave me alone! Ouch! My tail! A-h-h! it stings! My ears! Oh! Ah! It stings! Help, Help!

(Tiecelin enters.)

TIECELIN: Seigneur Brun! What is the matter?

BRUN: Out of my way, Crow! Ouch! My neck!

TIECELIN: Are you hurt?

BRUN: Am I hurt? I am eaten up! Aie! My leg! Stop blocking me! Oh, it stings! It stings!

(He runs off, followed by the bumble-bees. Tiecelin, pushed about, and stricken by fear, takes refuge on a tree. Reynard is convulsed.)

TIECELIN: Has he lost his mind?

REYNARD: Oh, no. He always acts that way, when the bees are after him.

TIECELIN: Well, he needn't be so rude about it. He nearly made me crush my camembert.

REYNARD: *(Nostrils wide open.)* Camembert? Ah, Master Crow, that cheese looks delicious. Will you give me a taste?

TIECELIN: No. I went to too much trouble to get it.

REYNARD: But cheese is bad for your voice. A singer should never eat cheese.

TIECELIN: Nonsense. It has never harmed me in the least.

REYNARD: Nevertheless, a fine voice should not be abused. If you were unable to sing any more, the animal kingdom would lose its best tenour.

TIECELIN: Do you think so?

(Crows.)

Do you really think so?

REYNARD: Sing, Tiecelin. Sing, and listen yourself.

(Tiecelin crows awfully.)

Ah! Very good, though a little low. I thought you could sing higher than that.

(Tiecelin croaks more shrilly.)

Better. One note higher . . . Ah! . . . More . . . Louder . . . Higher . . . Spendid! . . . Go on! . . . Higher! . . . You are almost there! Keep on! . . . More! . . . Now you have it!

(Tiecelin drops his cheese.)

And I have it too!

TIECELIN: My cheese!

REYNARD: Don't worry. It is in good hands.

TIECELIN: Give it back to me.

REYNARD: Come and get it.

TIECELIN: I know you.

REYNARD: We will share the cheese like brothers.

TIECELIN: If I come down, you will gobble me up first, and you will eat the cheese for dessert.

REYNARD: No, no. Come.

TIECELIN: Cheese robber!

REYNARD: What a wonderful aroma!

TIECELIN: Rob — you like the smell?

REYNARD: Heavenly!

TIECELIN: When you close your eyes, you find the smell even better.

REYNARD: What's that?

TIECELIN: To get the full, rich, luscious flavour of a camembert cheese, it is necessary to shut out all other senses, and enjoy it with your nose alone. Your nostrils are much more sensitive when your eyes are closed.

REYNARD: Is this possible?

(He closes his eyes and sniffs.)

You are right. It is unbelievably richer.

TIECELIN: *(Taking advantage of the chance to climb down.)* Cheese robber!

REYNARD: Tiecelin —

TIECELIN: This will go into my book!

REYNARD: Your book? What book?

TIECELIN: Aha! The King has appointed me to keep a record of all your doings in a book. This will make a fine beginning.

REYNARD: Indeed.

TIECELIN: Keep on, Master Fox. The book will soon be full. Crime Number One! Reynard stole my cheese! Cheese robber! Cheese robber! Cheese robber!

(*Exit.*)

REYNARD: So, he is keeping a book! And on the very first day of spring, I have managed to spend one of my twenty-four chances, and get it recorded in the book. Oh, what a stupid, bungling Fox I am! That tattle-tale will cry the news aloud, all through the forest. I'd better get rid of the evidence.

(*He hides cheese, as Noble enters, followed by Ysengrin.*)

NOBLE: Did you see a pheasant fly over?

REYNARD: No Sire, but I can guide your Majesty toward some very attractive turkeys.

YSENGRIN: Oh, no. You are out of this hunt, remember.

REYNARD: I am talking about big, fat turkeys.

NOBLE: We can hardly afford to let such a chance go by, Ysengrin.

YSENGRIN: But Sire, Reynard has given up hunting for a year. You said so, yourself.

NOBLE: I think — ahem! — we may make an exception this time.

REYNARD: This way, Sire.

(*Bows low. Noble and Ysengrin exeunt.*)

Let's hope that Tiecelin will not find his cheese until I get back.

(*Exit. Music. Ballet-mime for the hunt. Noble, Ysengrin, and Reynard chasing a turkey around the stage and off. Noble in the lead, graceful but heavy; Ysengrin lumbering along behind, eager but clumsy; Reynard nimbly outstripping both. The chase carries them offstage. Lendore enters.*)

LENDORE: (*Crossing, pillow under her arm.*) Impossible to sleep with this infernal music.

(*Exit. The ballet ends with the entrance of Reynard, who carries a turkey with head hanging limp. Noble and Ysengrin follow.*)

NOBLE: Bravo!

YSENGRIN: You caught it right under my nose!

REYNARD: It is a matter of skill, Cousin.

NOBLE: Anyhow, now we must share.

REYNARD: (*Throwing the turkey at Noble's feet.*) Let's share, by all means.

NOBLE: You, my dear Ysengrin, may decide about each one's share.

YSENGRIN: In my opinion, it is fitting, first of all, to set aside the claim of this redhair, who had no right to be hunting anyway. The head, the neck, and one wing will be enough for me — and one leg. It is only right that you, being the King, should take all the other pieces.

NOBLE: *(Boxing his ears.)* You don't have the first instinct of a sportsman.

(To Reynard.) And you, how would you divide it?

REYNARD: It is easy. Take first what pleases you, Sire — the body and legs, for instance. Her Majesty Lioness the Queen, shall have the wings and the head. Your son, the Cub, will gladly practice on the neck, I'm sure. Ysengrin seems to have too much trouble with his teeth to eat anything. And when it comes to me, I don't really feel hungry.

NOBLE: This is what I should call a fine division. Who taught you to divide so fairly?

REYNARD: My Fox's wisdom, Sire — and most of all, the sight of your royal fist on Ysengrin's ears.

NOBLE: I congratulate you. As for you, Seigneur Wolf, take a lesson from Reynard. Well, good bye, my friends. Thank you for your company in the hunt.

(Exit, taking turkey.)

YSENGRIN: Take a lesson — take a lesson from Reynard! Ah-h-h-h! I don't know what keeps me from giving you the beating of your life, you scheming, mealy-mouthed rascal!

REYNARD: Is that not better than to have your jaw crushed under the Lion's paw?

YSENGRIN: I am mad. Oh, I am good and mad!

REYNARD: Cheer up. We don't lose much in this settlement. The turkey was so old that the King, the Queen, and the Cub face the risk of breaking their teeth on it. Anyway, I see a much better dinner coming than the King's.

YSENGRIN: Epinard?

REYNARD: Yes, the Reverend, carrying a wonderful ham! It will be ours.

YSENGRIN: Beware the quills.

REYNARD: Don't worry about the quills. Hide there, and be on the watch. I'll get Epinard to lay the ham down near your hiding place. You pick it up and wait for me. Afterward we shall divide it.

YSENGRIN: Agreed.

(He hides.)

REYNARD: *(Waiting for Epinard's entrance.)* Now is the moment. Oh, miserable fox that I am!

(Epinard enters, carrying ham.)

Shall I never be able to do anything but bad deeds? With the help of Heaven, let me find a holy man to hear my confession, and absolve me of my sins!

EPINARD: My son.

REYNARD: Reverend. Did you hear me?

EPINARD: Yes, my son.

REYNARD: I will go to Hades, won't I?

EPINARD: The one who repents will not go to Hades.

REYNARD: Ah, but I repent. I repent.

EPINARD: Very well, my son.

REYNARD: Heavens, what do I see?

EPINARD: What do you see?

REYNARD: It has gotten me again.

EPINARD: What has gotten you again?

REYNARD: My terrible sin of greediness. Ah, how wretched am I! The very sight of your ham makes me forget my pledge.

EPINARD: Be calm, my son. Be calm.

REYNARD: It is impossible, Reverend, as long as that splendid ham remains before my eyes. I shall be unable not to covet it.

EPINARD: My goodness! Have some will power.

REYNARD: It is Satan. It is Satan who tempts me. "Get thee behind me, Satan." Take that ham away from my sight, Reverend, and pray for me.

(Epinard puts his ham down.)

Take it away from my nostrils — farther — still farther, so that its wonderful aroma will not tempt my nose any more.

EPINARD: *(Puts the ham down near Ysengrin's hiding place.)* Kneel, my son, my dear Reynard. Kneel. I will pray for you.

(Ysengrin seizes the ham, takes a bite, makes his escape. Reynard, seeing this, cries out involuntarily.)

REYNARD: Aie! Wait for me, you thief!

(Recovers himself.)

Excuse me, Reverend. Save the prayer for another time. Right now I have — ah — other business.

(Exit hurriedly, in pursuit of Ysengrin.)

EPINARD: *(Discovering his loss.)* Pig! Rascal! Robber! My ham! My ham!

(Exit. In the distance are heard the joined cries of Tiecelin — "Cheese Robber!" — and of Epinard — "My ham!" Noble enters.)

NOBLE: This morning the forest is full of strange sounds. Don't I hear someone claiming a ham? And somewhere, this side, someone else shouting "Cheese Robber"? That joker Reynard must not be far away. Ham? Cheese? It is strange, but I fancy my royal nose thrills under the odor of a very near camembert.

(He searches, and discovers the cheese.)

Ha! But I am not mistaken. By jove, my royal nose is still in its prime. Ah, this suits me admirably. It makes up for that skimpy breakfast I had, eating that tough old turkey.

(He eats the cheese.)

It is truly fit for a King.

TIECELIN: *(Offstage, drawing nearer.)* Cheese robber! Cheese robber!

(Noble gulps down the last of the cheese hurriedly. Tiecelin enters.)

Sire, my cheese.

NOBLE: What cheese?

TIECELIN: My camembert.

NOBLE: So it was your cheese that — ah — which is missing?

(Brun enters, shaking off Reynard behind him.)

BRUN: Don't give me any of your sweet talk. I am stung all over.

TIECELIN: He stole it!

NOBLE: Who? Brun?

TIECELIN: No, Sire. Reynard.

NOBLE: Reynard, did you sneal his wheeze?

REYNARD: Wheeze, Sire? No, Sire, I did not wheeze.

TIECELIN: Cheese robber! Cheese robber!

REYNARD: I did not wheeze. Nor did I hear anyone else wheeze, nor sneeze, nor queaze, nor —

TIECELIN: Cheese robber!

REYNARD: Oh, cheese? Tiecelin has lost a cheese?

TIECELIN: Your Majesty will do me justice. He has stolen my camembert.

REYNARD: Oh, what slander!

TIECELIN: Punish that thief.

REYNARD: Your Majesty, this Crow is insane. Had I stolen his cheese, I should have eaten it at once, and you would all be able to smell it. Uncle Brun, be good enough to smell my moustache.

BRUN: You stay away from me.

REYNARD: But smell, and tell us all. Do you detect the very strong odor of a camembert cheese?

BRUN: *(Sniffing)* I wouldn't put it past you, you honey-fibber — but to tell the truth, I smell nothing at all on your breath.

TIECELIN: You have taken it away from me!

REYNARD: After all, the simplest way would be to ask everyone to submit to the test, would it not?

NOBLE: Do you think this necessary?

TIECELIN: I insist! I insist!

BRUN: It seems logical to me. So smell.

TIECELIN: *(Smelling Brun's breath.)* You smell more like a honey-robber.

BRUN: It is my natural fragrance.

REYNARD: You, Sire?

NOBLE: Although my royal eminence places me above all suspicion, I submit to your insulting request.

TIECELIN: *(Smelling Noble's breath.)* Sire! Sire! One would almost think—

NOBLE: What would one think?

TIECELIN: If I weren't afraid of hurting your Majesty's feelings, I should say — it's funny, but it smells more or less like —

NOBLE: More or less like what?

TIECELIN: Like camembert.

NOBLE: This exceeds the limits. Get out of here, and go fast. Let me not set eyes on you any more today, or it might be costly for you.

TIECELIN: But —

NOBLE: Get out, I say!

TIECELIN: Very well, then.

(Exit.)

BRUN: What a fool!

TIECELIN: *(Offstage.)* Cheese robber! Cheese robber!

REYNARD: He has a one-track mind.

BRUN: How absurd to think that your Majesty's moustache might smell like cheese!

NOBLE: Sniff yourself, Seigneur Brun, and give us your opinion, sincerely and honestly.

BRUN: *(Sniffing.)* Uh — ah —

NOBLE: Well?

BRUN: I don't believe I am mistaken, Sire, when I say that your moustache does have an odor —

NOBLE: What odor, I pray you?

BRUN: A very delicate perfume — ah — yes, very similar to the roses.

NOBLE: So that is your honesty! Lies and hypocrisy! Out of my sight. Bear without conscience!

BRUN: Well, then —

(Exit, hastily.)

NOBLE: It is your turn, Reynard. What do you smell?

REYNARD: To tell the truth, Sire, I don't smell anything today. I have a cold in my head.

NOBLE: This is a cold that comes at a convenient time for you, doesn't it?

REYNARD: Yes, Sire.

EPINARD: *(In the distance.)* My ham! I claim my ham!

REYNARD: Sire, allow me to retire, and nurse my cold.

TIECELIN: *(In the distance, on the other side.)* Cheese robber! Cheese robber!

NOBLE: You are quite right. Let's both retire, and nurse our colds.

(Exeunt. Epinard enters.)

EPINARD: My ham!

(Tiecelin enters.)

TIECELIN: My cheese!

(Brun enters.)

BRUN: I am stung all over!

(Ysengrin enters.)

YSENGRIN: I am in the King's bad graces!

BRUN: So am I!

TIECELIN: So am I!

YSENGRIN: Whose fault is it?

TIECELIN: It is Reynard!

EPINARD: Reynard!

BRUN: Reynard!

TIECELIN: It is all the fault of that rascal Reynard!

EPINARD: Tiecelin, put all this down in your book against him.

TIECELIN: Don't worry. It shall go into my book, all right. H'm, h'm! We can almost be glad. This will make three crimes on the very first day. Ha, ha!

End of Scene One

Scene Two — Summer

(Appropriate music. Reynard is hidden behind a tree. Lendore and Epinard enter from opposite sides, both very thirsty, both looking for the spring. They collide.)

LENDORE: Oh, it's you?

EPINARD: As you see. Don't you think it's terribly hot?

LENDORE: Yes. Are you looking for the spring?

EPINARD: Where is it?

LENDORE: The hole is there, but the water doesn't flow any more. The brook has disappeared in the sand, the pond is dried up, and the fish, turned upside down, die in the sun.

EPINARD: May Heaven save us, dear Lendore! It is a dreadful summer.

(Ysengrin enters, brushes them aside.)

YSENGRIN: Out of the way, both of you!

(Epinard bristles. Lendore puts pillow on her head.)

Where is the spring? Who emptied the spring? You?

LENDORE: Certainly not. It is the sun.

YSENGRIN: I want a drink. Where is the water?

EPINARD: In the ground.

YSENGRIN: It must come out. I want it to gush, as it did before. Come out of your hole, water. I want a drink.

EPINARD: Don't shout so. Water doesn't hear. Each of us must be patient under our sufferings.

YSENGRIN: Don't preach your sermons to me. Go somewhere else.

(He pushes Epinard, stings himself.)

Thunderation!

EPINARD: As you wish.

(Exit calmly.)

LENDORE: He who plays with needles gets stung.

YSENGRIN: You think this is funny?

(Ysengrin strikes at Lendore, who pushes her pillow into his muzzle, and hurries off. Ysengrin fights alone with the pillow, as Brun enters, carrying a wooden bucket. He sets the bucket down, to watch Ysengrin in astonishment.)

BRUN: Here, don't upset my bucket!

YSENGRIN: What bucket?

(He throws the pillow down, and rushes to the bucket, kneeling in front of it.)

BRUN: *(Tumbles him down with a push.)* Don't touch!

YSENGRIN: Just a gulp.

BRUN: No.

YSENGRIN: I am thirsty.

BRUN: So am I.

YSENGRIN: I beg you.

BRUN: No.

YSENGRIN: One drop.

BRUN: No.

YSENGRIN: Only let me dip the tip of my tongue.

BRUN: No!

(He pushes Ysengrin back violently. Ysengrin tumbles down and rolls close to a tree, behind which Reynard is hidden. Brun drinks noisily. Reynard whispers a few secret words to Ysengrin, who then gets up and pretends to depart.)

Good bye, my nephew.

YSENGRIN: Good bye.

(He stops and pretends to gather honey, which he eats with delight.)

BRUN: *(Stops drinking to watch Ysengrin, then puts his bucket down and draws near.)* Is it honey?

(Reynard picks up the bucket and disappears.)

It is most probably honey?

YSENGRIN: No. I was just licking the wind.

(Exit, in pursuit of Reynard. Brun rushes for honey, finds none.)

BRUN: He *was* just licking the wind.

(Looks for his bucket.)

Ysengrin! Robber! Ysengrin! My bucket!

(Exit in pursuit. Reynard returns, drains the bucket, puts it back in place, then leaves. Ysengrin re-enters, rushes to the bucket, finds it empty.)

YSENGRIN: Scoundrel!

(Brun rushes in.)

BRUN: Give me that!

YSENGRIN: It is empty.

BRUN: *(Beating him.)* I'll teach you to rob your Uncle.

YSENGRIN: Uncle! Ouch! . . . Ouch! . . . I haven't — it isn't — oh, it is —

BRUN: Don't cross my path again, or you'll get twice as much.

(Exit. Reynard returns.)

REYNARD: Well? Do you have colic from drinking too much?

YSENGRIN: I have been beaten — through your fault. I am going to give you your share.

REYNARD: You are mistaken.

YSENGRIN: You have emptied the bucket, to the last drop.

REYNARD: Ah no! Is it my fault if there is a hole in the bucket?

YSENGRIN: Where?

REYNARD: Look!

(He puts the bucket on Ysengrin's head.)

YSENGRIN: Remove this bucket! I am smothering! Reynard, where are you?

REYNARD: I am here.

YSENGRIN: Get me out of this bucket at once!

REYNARD: Eat your way out. Remember, you ate Epinard's ham, all by yourself.

(Exit quietly.)

YSENGRIN: I'll strangle you! I'll pull out every hair of your moustache! I'll report this to Tiecelin to put in his book!

(Noble and Brun enter.)

BRUN: You see, Sire, the spring is dry.

NOBLE: Ah-h-h, yes.

BRUN: But I had the foresight to save back a bucket of water.

NOBLE: *(Panting.)* Where is it?

BRUN: That is what I am trying to tell you, Sire. I was tricked out of it.

NOBLE: Bah! Brun, I'm so thirsty I could drink the ocean.

BRUN: Drink the ocean?

NOBLE: I'd be willing to wager I could drink the ocean to the last drop.

YSENGRIN: *(Grapples with the King.)* Ah, villain, there you are!

NOBLE: *(Throwing him back so hard, it shakes the bucket.)* This will teach you to respect your King!

YSENGRIN: King? Oh, forgive me, Sire. I cannot see your Majesty.

NOBLE: Even if invisible, our Majesty is to be respected.

YSENGRIN: Take this bucket off my head, and I'll explain.

NOBLE: Quite unnecessary. I understand.

(Exit.)

YSENGRIN: Sire, I didn't rob Seigneur Brun. He jabbers a great deal lately.

BRUN: I, jabber?

(Gives him a mighty blow, and exit.)

YSENGRIN: Sire — your Majesty — will nobody help me?

(Lendore enters to pick up her pillow, notices Wolf. She knocks at the bucket discreetly.)

Who is there?

LENDORE: It's me, Lendore the Marmot, sir. And you, under the bucket, who are you?

YSENGRIN: I am the poor Ysengrin. For Heaven's sake, liberate me.

LENDORE: Promise first not to try to gobble me up again?

YSENGRIN: I promise anything, my sweet Lendore. I swear it a hundred times, a thousand times, if you wish. But remove this bucket. It is smothering me.

LENDORE: Don't move.

(She pulls at the bucket.)

YSENGRIN: You are pulling my ears off!

LENDORE: I have to.

YSENGRIN: *(Free, at last.)* You did hurt me!

LENDORE: It was unavoidable.

YSENGRIN: You deserve a thrashing.

LENDORE: Don't forget you swore —

YSENGRIN: Away with promises! Here is your reward.

(Trying to kick her, he misses, kicks the bucket instead. Lendore runs away. Ysengrin, in pain, hops on one foot. Tiecelin enters.)

Oh, I am in a rage — a rage — a rage!

TIECELIN: What is the matter with you? Have you lost one leg?

YSENGRIN: It is all the fault of that bounder Reynard!

TIECELIN: *(Eager, pencil poised.)* Reynard? What did he do? Tell me at once. I will put it in my book.

YSENGRIN: Your book? Your book? That for your book!

(He strikes the book from Tiecelin's hand.)

TIECELIN: *(Retrieving his book.)* Here, have a care!

YSENGRIN: Of what use is your everlasting book?

TIECELIN: It is a record of all his crimes, to bring against him at the trial.

YSENGRIN: Winter will be over before the trial. Are we to put up with his trickery till then?

TIECELIN: It is the King's judgement.

YSENGRIN: I want to deal with him now — right now!

TIECELIN: I, too. But how?

YSENGRIN: O, leave me in peace. I am lame for life!

TIECELIN: All the same, you needn't treat my book so lightly. This is legal evidence, sanctioned by the King. And it is getting full. He hasn't many chances left. If all else fails, this will bring him to account in the end.

(Exit.)

YSENGRIN: Prattling Crow!

(Reynard enters, but finding Ysengrin alone, conceals himself.)

It all goes back to the King's judgement. Leaving that Fox free for a year, to commit twenty-four crimes without punishment!

(Enter Brun.)

Uncle Brun!

BRUN: Don't speak to me, you water-thief!

YSENGRIN: But I beg you, listen to me. It was not I who emptied your bucket.

BRUN: Not you? Who, then?

YSENGRIN: It was Reynard.

BRUN: Reynard?

YSENGRIN: I swear it.

BRUN: Reynard, who drained my bucket dry?

YSENGRIN: And then stuck it on my head, and caused me to get a beating.

BRUN: The King shall hear of this!

YSENGRIN: Of what use is that? It was the King who set him free for a year, to perpetrate such tricks.

BRUN: And the year is not half over.

YSENGRIN: Exactly.

BRUN: It is not to be borne! We must put an end to this Fox!

YSENGRIN: If we are to get rid of the Fox, we must first get the King out of the way.

BRUN: The King is a fool. If I were King, now —

YSENGRIN: Or I —

BRUN: Why not?

YSENGRIN: Eh?

BRUN: Why should the Lion be King?

YSENGRIN: He always has been.

BRUN: Do you know any document that gives the title of King of the animals to the Lion?

YSENGRIN: All the school books say so.

BRUN: I know a way to topple him off his throne.

YSENGRIN: What way?

BRUN: Listen. This afternoon, his Majesty declared several times that he could drink the entire ocean, to the last drop.

YSENGRIN: That was only to express how thirsty he was.

BRUN: Of course. But what would happen if we should challenge him?

YSENGRIN: He would naturally be most embarrassed. I don't see how he could very well drink the ocean dry.

BRUN: Well, then! Do you think the animal kingdom will accept a King who is unable to keep his word?

YSENGRIN: No!

BRUN: No! Certainly not! We shall demand his abdication.

YSENGRIN: And take the throne ourselves!

BRUN: Tonight, my friend, we shall be Kings.

YSENGRIN: And we shall make an end of that rascal Reynard. Go and get him. I will gather the Court.

BRUN: Reynard has played his last trick.

(Exit.)

YSENGRIN: And that for you, Master Reynard. Trumpets!

(Trumpets. Reynard appears in the open, pretending to answer the trumpet call.)

REYNARD: Cousin, what is going on?

YSENGRIN: You'll see. Trumpets!

(Trumpets. Tiecelin enters.)

TIECELIN: Why are you calling a meeting when it is so hot? It must be most important.

(Trumpets. Enter Lendore.)

YSENGRIN: It certainly is. Trumpets!

LENDORE: There, there. Everybody has heard you. What is the matter now?

YSENGRIN: The King has made a very audacious boast, and he wants everybody present to see how he keeps it.

(Noble sweeps in, escorted by Brun.)

NOBLE: What is all this congregation for?

TIECELIN: The trumpets have called us to Assembly. I, as Royal Registrar, demand to know the business before the Court.

BRUN: You shall know it now. Sire, the animal kingdom, whose beloved sovereign you are, wishes to know if it is possible for your Majesty to keep a promise made by you this afternoon.

NOBLE: Why, certainly.

BRUN: Would you be willing to put your throne at stake?

NOBLE: Of course I would. I always keep my promises. What did I promise?

BRUN: To drink the ocean, Sire.

NOBLE: Ha, ha! It is true I made that statement, I was so thirsty.

YSENGRIN: The achievement you are going to perform thrills all your people, Sire.

NOBLE: You didn't take me seriously, I hope?

BRUN: We know your Majesty capable of accomplishing the greatest feats.

NOBLE: But you know very well —

YSENGRIN: Your people are looking forward to it, Sire.

BRUN: Gentlemen, your highly esteemed sovereign will, in a moment, lead you to the beach, and show you how, when one is a very great King, one can achieve things that would be impossible for his subjects.

YSENGRIN: His Majesty is going to drink the ocean.

BRUN: You will see how the strength of your sovereign, his bravery, his keen intelligence, his wit, and his determination will give him the power to drink the whole ocean. Our great King, gentlemen, is about to swallow the ocean. Sire, the ocean is waiting.

NOBLE: Did I actually say that I would drink the ocean?

BRUN: Indeed you did, Sire — to the last drop.

NOBLE: Did I say that?

BRUN: Those were your very words, Sire.

NOBLE: But — but I shall drown!

BRUN: Does your Majesty mean you cannot keep your promise?

NOBLE: I — ah —

YSENGRIN: A King always keeps his promises.

NOBLE: But it was only in jest —

REYNARD: Ah — your Majesty. Gentlemen.

YSENGRIN: You stay out of this.

REYNARD: Did the King also say that he would drink the water of all the rivers that flow into the ocean?

BRUN: Is this any business of yours?

NOBLE: No. I did not.

REYNARD: In that case, my dear Brun, will you stop all the rivers of the world, dam their flow, and prevent them from pouring their waters into his Majesty's soup? After you have done this, I'm sure his Majesty will gladly drink what is left.

BRUN: Stop up all the rivers of the world?

NOBLE: Exactly.

BRUN: How can anyone do that?

NOBLE: When you are able to do that, I will drink up all the waters of the ocean, to the last drop.

(General laughter.)

REYNARD: Bravo, Sire. It is easy to see that we have a wise King. Don't you agree, Cousin Ysengrin?

YSENGRIN: It is easy to see that the King has a clever counsellor.

BRUN: Counsellor? This redhair? Your Majesty, this is an outrage, that you should be taken in by this rogue!

NOBLE: Rogue? Are you referring to my trusted knight, Sir Reynard the Fox? Guard your tongue, Seigneur Bear.

BRUN: Only today he tricked me out of a bucket of water.

(Tiecelin writes busily.)

YSENGRIN: And then he inverted the bucket on my head, and caused me to get a beating.

(Tiecelin writes this down too.)

NOBLE: *(To Brun.)* You dare complain to me, when you have just tried to cheat me out of my throne?

(To Ysengrin.) And you, who just this afternoon, without provocation, assaulted your King? Let me hear not another word from either one of you. Come, Reynard. A rain is coming up. Let us seek shelter.

(Epinard rushes in.)

EPINARD: Sire! I beg — a matter of utmost importance!

BRUN: Save your important matters for the pulpit, Reverend.

EPINARD: Sire, give me leave to —

NOBLE: In good time, Reverend.

EPINARD: Your Majesty, it cannot wait. Does no one realize that a very serious danger threatens us all?

NOBLE: What danger can be greater than this wicked plot to overthrow my throne?

EPINARD: Men, Sire.

LENDORE: Men?

(The very word draws them together, in a tight little knot, glancing fearfully toward the overlook.)

EPINARD: Sire, I have just come from the farm. The farmer has his hunting dogs out on a leash, training them to pick up our scent.

NOBLE: How do you know this?

EPINARD: He led the dogs first to the hen-yard, where Reynard was careless enough to leave some tracks. Then he took them to the marshes, where I — ahem! — paid a brief call on some ducks recently. When I left, he was heading toward the pig-pen, where the dogs will easily pick up the trail of Seigneur Brun.

BRUN: The dickens!

EPINARD: From there, he will take them to the sheep-fold, where the smell of Wolf is very strong.

YSENGRIN: Oh, no!

EPINARD: Next they will go to the wheat field, where the Crow dropped a feather on his last visit.

TIECELIN: Aie!

EPINARD: And finally they will make for the pasture, where the Lion has left his traces.

NOBLE: Is this true?

EPINARD: Send Tiecelin to see.

NOBLE: Tiecelin, to the farm!

TIECELIN: A-a-a-alone, Sire?

NOBLE: Have we anybody else with wings?

TIECELIN: Y-y-yes, Sire. I mean — no, Sire.

NOBLE: Quickly!

TIECELIN: I — I'm going, Sire.

(Exit slowly, with obvious reluctance.)

EPINARD: Your Majesty, this is no time for nonsense. I know those farmers down there. They are all united in plotting our destruction. They want our bodies; the pelt of Seigneur Brun; Reynard's fur; Tiecelin's feathers; Ysengrin's skin and teeth; yours, Sire; my quills — and Heaven knows what else. Fall is coming, when all men go hunting for game. The dogs have our scent. Men are polishing up their weapons, oiling their rifles, filling their cartridges, sharpening their knives. It will be a fearful period for those of our kind. I make it my duty, Sire, to warn you that if we wish to survive, we must all band together against the common enemy — Man.

REYNARD: That, Reverend, is one of your very best sermons.

EPINARD: Thank you.

NOBLE: You agree, then?

REYNARD: Oh, unquestionably, your Majesty. Alone, we are each of us weak and vulnerable. United, we could resist the hunters and their dogs.

NOBLE: But how can we unite?

REYNARD: Ah! That, Sire, is the question.

NOBLE: It is always the question. I am going to require each of you to take an oath.

EPINARD: Excellent, Sire.

NOBLE: And I will expect you to be bound by this oath, no matter what the emergency.

YSENGRIN: Never fear, Sire. You can depend on us.

NOBLE: Hold out your right hands. Now, repeat after me. All for one. One for all.

ALL: All for one. One for all.

(Low, distant rumble of thunder. All are frozen.)

YSENGRIN: Listen!

(Tiecelin flies in, terrified.)

TIECELIN: Did you hear that?

YSENGRIN: It's gunfire.

BRUN: The hunters! The hunters are after us!

LENDORE: Merciful heavens! Already?

(A loud thunder-clap.)

TIECELIN: Hunters? That is cannon!

YSENGRIN: They've brought in the Army!

BRUN: The Army? Soldiers?

TIECELIN: The soldiers are coming!

LENDORE: E-e-e-ek!

REYNARD: It is only thunder, Sire.

BRUN: Thunder?

(*Violent cracks, as the storm breaks.*)

Sire, this redhair doesn't know the difference between gunfire and thunder.

YSENGRIN: It is the hunters!

TIECELIN: It is the soldiers!

REYNARD: Gentlemen, calm yourselves. It is simply thunder.

NOBLE: Hunters, soldiers, or thunder — I am taking no chances. Excuse me, gentlemen.

(*Exit, hurriedly.*)

TIECELIN: Your Majesty! Wait for me!

(*Tiecelin, Brun, and Ysengrin collide in their scramble to run for safety.*)

BRUN: Out of my way, Crow!

(*Tiecelin exits in a panic.*)

YSENGRIN: No you don't. Me first!

(*Exit.*)

LENDORE: Where is everybody going?

BRUN: It is the hunters! Save yourself!

(*Exit, on the run.*)

LENDORE: The hunters? Oh, help me!

(*Clings fearfully to Epinard as he rushes past, on his way to the overlook.*)

EPINARD: Help you? Each one help himself!

LENDORE: But we just promised — All for one. One for all.

REYNARD: Only when convenient, Lendore.

EPINARD: Ah! You were right, Reynard. It was only thunder, after all. And here comes the rain.

LENDORE: Rain?

REYNARD: Yes, Lendore. Use your pillow for an umbrella.

EPINARD: These thunder-showers bring out the snails. You understand? I must be on the watch for them.

(*Exit hastily.*)

REYNARD: Of course, Reverend.

LENDORE: But the Reverend is the one who said we must unite.

REYNARD: Ah, yes, Lendore. And yet, you see, at the first thunder-stroke, he goes off in his own interest, like everybody else.

LENDORE: But suppose it *had* been the hunters?

REYNARD: You and I would have been left to meet them, alone.

LENDORE: *(Hastening out)* Heavens! Not me!

(Exit.)

REYNARD: Then it is Reynard alone against the hunters. Let them come! Even the rain is on my side. It will wash away my tracks, so the dogs can no longer pick up my trail. Let it rain! Ha, ha! It is a good joke on Man!

End of Scene Two

Scene Three — Autumn

(Music. Sounds of gaiety and merriment from the distant vineyard. Epinard stands at the overlook, peering off toward the farm. Lendore enters cautiously, carrying a basket.)

LENDORE: Greetings, Reverend. Is it safe to gather my supplies here?

EPINARD: For the present. Men are still busy celebrating.

LENDORE: Blessed be God who created the autumn.

EPINARD: It is the harvest season, my dear Lendore. You can see the wine-growers' dance from here. Men are full of joy, for the grapes are ripe.

LENDORE: So are the pears and apples, and the nuts and acorns. They will make a good crop to fill my attic.

EPINARD: As long as men are dancing, we are safe. But as soon as the harvest is over, they will take down their guns, call their dogs, and sound the horn. Then our only salvation will be to flee into the heart of the forest, and hide. May Heaven help us when they blow the horn!

LENDORE: Yes. Well, meanwhile, give me a hand in gathering my provisions.

(They start out, but encounter Brun coming in.)

BRUN: Do you have to take up the whole path?

LENDORE: No, but I wish you would watch where you step. You just crushed a chestnut.

(Exit.)

BRUN: You and your chestnuts! I have an appointment with the Royal Registrar.

EPINARD: Don't venture out into the open. Men are about.

BRUN: Men?

EPINARD: You can see them from there.

(Exit. Brun goes to the overlook. Tiecelin enters.)

TIECELIN: The Royal Registrar is not accustomed to be kept waiting, Master Brun.

BRUN: Look — Men!

TIECELIN: *(Looking.)* It is the wine-growers' dance.

BRUN: Don't let them see you.

TIECELIN: Do you take me for a dunce?

(Ysengrin enters.)

YSENGRIN: Brun! Tiecelin! I have been looking for you.

TIECELIN: Men are dancing, Ysengrin.

40

YSENGRIN: Men?

BRUN: They are celebrating the harvest.

TIECELIN: Don't show yourself. From now on, we shall have to stay under cover.

YSENGRIN: I will not be hedged into this forest all winter with that rascally Fox!

BRUN: Nor I!

TIECELIN: Gentlemen, take heart. Do you know how many counts I have accumulated against him in my book? Twenty-two!

YSENGRIN: But the year is only half over!

BRUN: Are we to suffer through the fall and winter, without any respite from his tricks?

TIECELIN: Do you have anything else to suggest?

YSENGRIN: Yes!

BRUN: Eh?

YSENGRIN: I have a new plan to dispose of the Fox!

BRUN: Now?

YSENGRIN: Now!

BRUN: Without waiting for Tiecelin's book to fill up?

YSENGRIN: Without waiting one more day.

BRUN and TIECELIN: We are listening.

YSENGRIN: Suppose I should convince the King that the lower classes — the pheasants, the ducks, geese, turkeys, chickens, rabbits, pigeons, and mice — have chosen me as their defender, and have charged me to challenge Reynard to a duel.

BRUN: Yes?

YSENGRIN: If you two should back me up, with all the prestige of your position, the King would not be in position to refuse the fight, and I should make a quick end to the redhair. You know me.

BRUN: Good! Eh, Tiecelin?

TIECELIN: Why didn't you think of this sooner? You could have saved me a lot of trouble.

BRUN: We'll help you. But if you give that Fox half a chance, he will turn the tables. I want all the chances to be on your side.

YSENGRIN: The chances *are* on my side. I am the best swordsman in the kingdom.

BRUN: Nevertheless, I will provide the swords. Reynard's will be so skill-fully made, that it will break at the first stroke.

YSENGRIN: I can win without such trickery.

BRUN: Some caution is necessary, my dear nephew. Follow my advice, and Reynard will be out of our way soon. I will go fix the swords. You inform the King.

(Exit.)

YSENGRIN: Do I need this treachery? Am I not stronger and braver than Reynard?

TIECELIN: You are, and without flattery, Seigneur Wolf. But nobody is as tricky as he is.

YSENGRIN: Tiecelin, you are a man of law. Give me your advice. Do you think it is honest and fair to allot him a faked weapon?

TIECELIN: As for being fair, certainly not. Honest — even less so. But as for being smart — ha, ha!

YSENGRIN: Do you think so?

TIECELIN: A trick is just what that Fox deserves!

YSENGRIN: But this one will cost him his skin.

TIECELIN: Isn't that what you wish? Besides, so do I.

YSENGRIN: Then consider it done. You may throw away your book, Tiecelin.

TIECELIN: Throw away my book? This book is going into history! Throw away my book, indeed!

YSENGRIN: As you wish. But we shall make an end of Reynard without it. I am going to arrange this matter with the King. As for you, not a word about this.

(Exit.)

TIECELIN: Count on me, Seigneur. This time Reynard shall definitely be punished.

(Epinard enters.)

EPINARD: Who is going to punish Reynard? You?

TIECELIN: That, Reverend, is a secret. I promised —

EPINARD: Oh, very well. I don't insist.

(Goes to the overlook to watch the wine-growers' dance.)

TIECELIN: Reverend —

EPINARD: Still dancing. Did you call me?

TIECELIN: If I told you that secret —

EPINARD: That wouldn't be very proper, would it? . . . I am listening.

TIECELIN: Ysengrin is going to challenge Reynard to a duel.

EPINARD: Is that a secret?

TIECELIN: No, but what is one — and it is this I beg you to keep secret — is that Reynard's sword will be faked.

EPINARD: Faked?

TIECELIN: It will break in two, at the first stroke.

EPINARD: That is certainly not fair, but it is fitting.

TIECELIN: Do you think so, too?

EPINARD: That scamp has tricked me out of a ham, and a duck-egg. He doesn't deserve any better.

TIECELIN: I couldn't agree with you more.

(Trumpet off.)

The King is calling me.

(He starts out.)

Not a word. It is a secret.

(Exit.)

EPINARD: *(Alone.)* It was bound to turn out this way. Reynard has so often fooled the rest of us. Now it is his turn to be fooled.

(Enter Lendore.)

LENDORE: See how much I have gathered?

EPINARD: We gather what we sow, and I pity — yes, I deeply pity the one who has sown bad seed.

LENDORE: Who has sown bad seed?

EPINARD: Reynard.

LENDORE: Has Reynard been planting seeds?

EPINARD: He has spread the spirit of trickery among the animals, and he will be destroyed by trickery.

LENDORE: Is someone going to destroy Reynard?

EPINARD: Ysengrin is calling for a duel with him.

LENDORE: The Wolf is strong, of course, but Reynard is shrewd.

EPINARD: He cannot escape this time. In fact, my dear Lendore, I will tell you — but for Goodness' sake, don't repeat it to anyone. Reynard will soon meet his end, for his sword will be faked. It will break in two at the first stroke.

LENDORE: Oh, no!

EPINARD: It is a secret, Lendore. Don't tell anybody.

(Exit.)

LENDORE: It is wrong just the same. Oh! They all agreed we should unite against Men — and that was right. But we should also unite against those who fake swords.

(Enter Reynard.)

REYNARD: Who fakes swords?

LENDORE: Reynard, I will tell you, because foul play is wrong.

REYNARD: Foul play?

LENDORE: Ysengrin is going to challenge you to a duel.

REYNARD: Ho! I am equal to that kind of trap.

LENDORE: That is not all. They will provide you with a faked sword. It will break in two at the first stroke. Ysengrin will kill you.

REYNARD: That remains to be seen.

TIECELIN: *(Offstage.)* Reynard! Reynard the Redhair! Where are you?

REYNARD: Here comes the messenger of death. Leave me, Lendore — and thanks, old friend.

LENDORE: Don't forget. It is a secret.

(Exit.)

TIECELIN: *(Offstage.)* Reynard the Redhair!

REYNARD: What do you want with me?

(Tiecelin enters.)

TIECELIN: Stay where you are. Trumpets!

(Trumpets.)

Royal message! By order of the King — stay there! His Majesty Noble the Lion — don't move! We, Tiecelin the Crow, Royal Registrar — stop! — request the Knight Reynard to hold himself at the disposal of the King, in order to meet in a duel the accuser, Ysengrin the Wolf, Marshall of the Court, and defender of the lower class. Let it be known! Signed, Noble the Lion, King of the animals. Trumpets!

(Trumpets.)

REYNARD: Is that all? Pouf, it is not much. Tell your master that Reynard is ready.

(Noble enters.)

NOBLE: Come, Tiecelin, if we have to have this duel, let's get it over. Sound the call.

TIECELIN: Yes, Sire. Trumpets!

(Trumpets. The offstage festival gaiety dies away.)

REYNARD: Hail, oh Noble Sire Lion, the wisest and bravest among us all.

NOBLE: Greetings, Knight Reynard. You already know the reason for my royal call.

REYNARD: I know, Sire.

(Ysengrin enters.)

YSENGRIN: I humbly greet your Royal Majesty.

NOBLE: Greetings, Seigneur Ysengrin.

(Epinard enters.)

EPINARD: God keep you, gentlemen.

NOBLE: Knight Reynard, Marshall Ysengrin has been chosen the champion of the lower class, and I am compelled — against my will, believe me — to grant him the duel he calls for. As weapon, your Cousin has chosen the sword.

(Enter Brun, with two swords.)

BRUN: Here are the weapons, Sire.

NOBLE: You have the choice, Ysengrin.

(Brun openly hands Ysengrin the sword prepared for him.)

YSENGRIN: *(Pretending to select.)* I'll take this one, the shorter.

BRUN: Here is yours, Reynard.

REYNARD: *(Takes the sword without looking at it.)* Your Majesty, I cannot accept this weapon.

BRUN: Why not?

YSENGRIN: What does this mean?

NOBLE: Do you refuse to fight?

REYNARD: I am not a champion, your Majesty. I am unworthy to fight Ysengrin with a sword.

(He breaks the sword across his knee.)

NOBLE: What do you mean?

REYNARD: Sire, Ysengrin represents the lower classes, and fights as their champion. I am defending nobody but myself, a poor Fox. I will be satisfied with a Fox's weapon. Attendant!

(Lendore enters, carrying a stick.)

Here, Sire, is my weapon.

NOBLE: This is not customary, but I don't think the Marshall will object?

YSENGRIN: I agree. But under the circumstances, I require the use of a shield.

NOBLE: Granted.
(Brun brings a heavy iron shield.)

REYNARD: My shield!

(Lendore hands him her pillow.)

NOBLE: Do you expect to fight in this attire?

REYNARD: It is good enough for me, Sire.

NOBLE: As you wish, though I think this whole thing is absurd. Gentlemen, take your places. The fight will start when I give the signal, after three trumpet calls. It is strictly forbidden for anyone to interfere in the fight. On guard, Knights, and let the noblest be victorious!

ALL: Let the noblest be victorious!

TIECELIN: Trumpets!

(Trumpets. The opponents eye each other.)

Trumpets!

(Trumpets. Each one raises his shield and gets ready.)

Trumpets!

(Trumpets.)

NOBLE: Go!

(Music. Ballet-mime. Long duel, during which Reynard's cunning is matched against Ysengrin's strength. Reynard uses the pillow as much as the stick. Ysengrin gets nervous and loses his balance. Any impulse on the part of spectators to take Ysengrin's side is sternly frowned down by the King. After several phases, Reynard, with a masterful pillow blow, tumbles Ysengrin to the ground. Immediately he puts his foot on Ysengrin's shield, as a token of victory, and greets the King with his stick. Ysengrin, taking advantage of this moment of inattention, lifts his shield violently, throwing Reynard down, and making him drop his stick and pillow. Ysengrin leaps up and puts his foot on Reynard's chest, threatening him with his sword.)

BRUN: *(Quickly.)* Ysengrin is the winner!

NOBLE: But only a moment ago —

EPINARD: Heaven has judged.

TIECELIN: His Majesty will declare Ysengrin the winner!

NOBLE: *(Reluctantly.)* Seigneur Ysengrin, I proclaim you Reynard's conqueror. His life belongs to you.

YSENGRIN: I want him to hang. But first of all, I want him humiliated in front of all — to beg forgiveness for his crimes. After that, he shall die.

REYNARD: Oh, Ysengrin, you are truly generous, to give me the opportunity to confess my sins, and beg forgiveness. Let me confess privately to each of you, and ask your blessing.

NOBLE: Granted, my poor Reynard. Come, gentlemen, let us make it possible for Reynard to unburden his conscience.

BRUN: That Fox will find a way to escape, if we give him such a chance.

NOBLE: If you are afraid of that, Seigneur Brun, you may keep watch on the east side, and Ysengrin will guard the west. I myself will take care of the north.

EPINARD: *(Indicating the auditorium.)* Do you wish me to watch the south?

NOBLE: It is not necessary, Reverend. The forest is impenetrable, this side. Who will be the first to hear your confession?

REYNARD: Lendore, if you will allow it.

NOBLE: Granted. Let's go, gentlemen. And keep watch.

(All leave, except Lendore and Reynard.)

LENDORE: My poor Reynard.

REYNARD: *(On his knees.)* Draw nearer, Lendore, and receive my confession.

(Whispers.) Look as stern as you can, and open your ears.

LENDORE: *(Loudly.)* Go on, wretched scoundrel. Unload your conscience, and don't dally.

REYNARD: *(Whispering.)* You must get me out of this fix.

LENDORE: All the roads of escape are guarded.

REYNARD: If I cannot run away, we must make *them* do it. Go out and find a loud instrument somewhere, to make a big noise. Imitate the barking of dogs. Make a monstrous uproar. If you can make them think the hunters are here, they will run away. Do you understand?

LENDORE: You can count on me.

REYNARD: Give me your blessing, good and loud, for their benefit. Thanks, old friend, and don't fall asleep on your way. Hurry back!

LENDORE: One for all, all for one.

(Exit.)

REYNARD: Next, Ysengrin.

(Ysengrin approaches.)

YSENGRIN: Well, Master Joker. Are you expecting you to receive our pardon?

REYNARD: Ysengrin, I acknowledge that I fully deserve the fate that lies in store for me.

YSENGRIN: Oh, yes?

REYNARD: Yes. And besides, if I had to lose, I'm glad to lose to so brave an adversary.

YSENGRIN: Enough hypocrisy!

REYNARD: I don't want to leave this world without proving that I hold no grudge against you for your victory. A short while ago, I spotted an easy and very appetizing prey. How would you like to benefit from it, since I shall not be here any more?

YSENGRIN: Is this your confession?

REYNARD: How would you feel about a plump hen?

YSENGRIN: Easy to catch?

REYNARD: Child's play. Every night she takes a walk right here, looking for her rooster. Just hide over there when twilight comes, imitate the rooster's cry, and the hen will come to you trustingly. You can make short work of her, if you strike her down with a heavy stick. Hit well and hit hard, for she is tough to kill, they say. That hen, Cousin, ought to be worth your benediction.

YSENGRIN: Yes. Pax vobiscum.

(Exit.)

REYNARD: Next, Uncle Brun.

(Enter Brun.)

BRUN: Not hanged yet?

REYNARD: In good time, Uncle.

BRUN: I shall not be sorry for it.

REYNARD: I will not beg your pardon, for I have done you too much wrong, but let me be remembered for one last good turn. Would you like a good meal?

BRUN: Is it another bumble-bee's nest?

REYNARD: Don't talk so loudly. It is a wonderful rooster. Each night, he strolls right here, looking for his hen. Just hide over there, and imitate her cackling to lure the rooster. It will be child's play for you to strike him down with a heavy stick. Hit well and hit hard, for he is tough to kill, they say.

BRUN: Is this not a new trap?

REYNARD: Uncle! How can you think I would play you a trick at the moment I am going to die? No. I wish you good appetite, and ask your blessing.

BRUN: Go in peace. And may the rope be quickly ready, so you may go soon.

(Exit.)

REYNARD: Thank you, Uncle. Don't forget. Over there, when twilight comes.

(To himself.) What the dickens can be keeping Lendore?

(Aloud.) Next, Sire.

(Noble enters.)

NOBLE: Reynard, I was maneuvered into this, and now I am powerless to help you.

REYNARD: Rest easy, Sire. I attach no blame to you. Let me only take this last chance to thank you, Sire, for your many kindnesses —

NOBLE: Oh, Reynard, how am I to do without you!

REYNARD: I am only a wicked Fox, Sire.

NOBLE: You are the only honest rogue among us all. Why did you let yourself in for this? Don't you know they will not rest until they have your life? See, here is Brun, with the rope.

(Brun enters, with tying-rope.)

BRUN: Sire, the time has come to tie him up.

REYNARD: *(To himself.)* And still Lendore has not come back.

(The company re-gathers on stage. Brun ties Reynard's hands.)

YSENGRIN: *(Brings hanging-rope, flings it over tree-limb.)* Next. You, Reynard.

REYNARD: *(Tied.)* Here I am. May God have mercy on me, a miserable Fox, who was led by demons to the most dreadful crimes.

BRUN: Hang him quick, and let us forget about it.

REYNARD: But where is Lendore?

BRUN: She is gone.

REYNARD: I would like to hug her one more time.

YSENGRIN: Don't let us wait any longer, Sire.

REYNARD: May I not see her once more?

BRUN: Can't you see he is only trying to gain time?

REYNARD: She was my true friend.

BRUN: Ah, well, let's put an end to this.

TIECELIN: Hang him!

(Ysengrin pulls the rope, experimentally. At this moment, there is the sound of a hunting-horn.)

BRUN: Men!

EPINARD: *(Rushing to look.)* They have stopped dancing!

(An outbreak of dog-barks, offstage.)

YSENGRIN: Dogs!

TIECELIN: Hunting dogs!

BRUN: On the chase!

(A dramatic explosion of rapid-fire, staccato bangs.)

EPINARD: It is the hunt!

NOBLE: The hunt is on! Take cover!

(Noble flees.)

TIECELIN: Escape if you can!

(Exit, flying. General flight.)

YSENGRIN: *(Holding Reynard's hanging-rope.)* Wait! Wait! We must hang him!

BRUN: Come! Do you wish to get pulled apart by dogs?

(Exit.)

YSENGRIN: *(Torn, he starts off, hesitates.)* But —

(Another burst of rapid-fire bangs, accompanied by barking.)

Farewell, Master Reynard. The dogs will take care of you.

(Exit.)

REYNARD: *(Alone.)* Lendore was a true friend.

(Lendore enters, beating a saucepan, blowing a hunting-horn, and barking.)

LENDORE: Woof! Woof! Bow-wow! Bow-wow!

(She laughs.)

Ha, ha, ha! I never saw them run so fast!

REYNARD: Thanks, my dear. It was high time.

LENDORE: *(Releasing him from the rope, and untying his bonds.)* You'll never know the trouble I had to find this horn, and this saucepan.

REYNARD: My good friend, I must be off.

LENDORE: Where will you go?

REYNARD: I will have to make for the outer edge of the woods.

LENDORE: *(Concerned.)* But that is where the men do their hunting.

REYNARD: If I can elude this pack of rascals, I can surely stay out of the reach of men.

LENDORE: Take care, Reynard.

REYNARD: I will need a little time to get away. If you will be good enough to keep up the music a few moments —

LENDORE: Oh, gladly!

REYNARD: Good bye, old friend.

(Lendore gleefully beats, blows, and barks, though her barking turns a little plaintive, as she watches Reynard go. As she goes out the opposite side, her noise retreats, and soon gives way to the renewed sounds of celebration in the distant vineyard. Lights dim slowly, leaving the empty stage in twilight. Cautiously, Tiecelin peers around a bush, then creeps in.)

TIECELIN: *(Alone.)* The rope is empty. Reynard is gone. But where is the hunt?

(Music and laughter from the vineyard. Tiecelin runs to look.)

They are dancing again. Ah-h-h! It was all a hoax! There were no hunters. There were no horns. There were no dogs. There was only noise. Reynard has fooled us once again. Oh, that wily Fox! He has out-tricked Ysengrin. He has out-tricked Brun. But he will not out-trick me. I still have my book. And this will make his twenty-third crime!

(Exit. A moment of music. Night falls. Semi-darkness with light background, so that the following scene may be played in silhouette. Ysengrin enters, right side, with stick.)

YSENGRIN: This is the place where Reynard told me to look for that hen. Kikikiki —

(Brun enters, left side, armed with club.)

BRUN: Cluck, cluck, cluck —

YSENGRIN: Kikiriki —

(They advance slowly toward each other.)

BRUN: Hold still, you rooster!

YSENGRIN: Rooster? How dare you call me a rooster! Take that, you miserable hen!

BRUN: Hen? Is this a hen stroke?

(They fight in earnest, and quickly discover each other at the same time.)

Ysengrin! So you want to fight, do you?

YSENGRIN: Brun! What are you beating me for?

BRUN: *(Chasing him.)* I'll show you what a beating is!

YSENGRIN: *(Fleeing.)* Help! Help!

(From the distant vineyard comes a burst of laughter.)

End of Scene Three

Scene IV — Winter

(Music. Wind. In the distance the howling of the Wolf can be heard. Stage lights come up slowly. Tiecelin, shivering, is stamping his feet.

Brun enters, muffled up in his fur.)

TIECELIN: It is winter, Master Brun.

BRUN: You don't have to tell me.

TIECELIN: Here we are, huddled together in a tight little circle, with fortifications all around us. We don't even have any place to run, to keep warm.

BRUN: Hug yourself with your feathers.

TIECELIN: I have tried that, but my feathers are cold, too. And the frost has made the ground so hard that it doesn't provide food any more. I am hungry, Seigneur Brun, and I am not the only one. Listen to the Wolf. What bitter cold! The pool is covered with ice, and even my tongue is frozen, and stiff as a stick.

BRUN: If you kept your mouth shut, this wouldn't happen.

TIECELIN: I would gladly shut it on some food, wouldn't you?

(Lendore crosses slowly, pillow under her arm, overwhelmed with sleep.)

Where are you going?

LENDORE: To sleep.

(Noble enters, overcome by a comic cough.)

NOBLE: Find me a doctor. Promise him a fourth, even half of my kingdom, but let him release me from this awful cough.

TIECELIN: A doctor? Where are we to find a doctor?

BRUN: We are holed up here like fugitives.

TIECELIN: Beyond the barricade, hunting dogs are waiting to pounce on us.

BRUN: And behind them are the hunters with their guns.

TIECELIN: None of us dares to stick our nose beyond the barricade.

NOBLE: But this is a matter of life or death.

TIECELIN: Your Majesty only has a bad cold.

NOBLE: Bad cold? Your King is dying of pneumonia, and there is no one here to lift a finger. Oh, where is Reynard!

TIECELIN: Reynard? The redhair!

NOBLE: Yes. Oh, my good Reynard, if you were only here!

TIECELIN: Your Majesty surely would not wish such a thing.

BRUN: He'd better not show his face around here.

NOBLE: Find him. Search the kingdom!

TIECELIN: Outside the barricade, where the dogs are lurking?

NOBLE: Even to the edge of the forest!

BRUN: The edge of the forest, where men are waiting with their guns?

TIECELIN: Would you have us risk our lives?

NOBLE: Yes! Bring me Reynard.

TIECELIN: Your Majesty, Reynard is in hiding. He would not dare to come.

BRUN: He knows a hanging is waiting for him.

NOBLE: Tell him I will forgive him everything, if he will only come back.

(Lendore exits quietly, but purposefully.)

BRUN: Forgive him?

TIECELIN: Forgive him all the crimes he has committed against us?

BRUN: Forgive him this rope?

TIECELIN: It is beyond your power, Sire. My book is full of indictments against him — twenty-four, to be exact.

NOBLE: Then I am doomed. Only Reynard can find a way to save me.

(Ysengrin enters, starving, violent.)

YSENGRIN: Give me something to eat — no matter what, but something.

NOBLE: I am sick, Ysengrin.

YSENGRIN: And I am hungry, Sire.

TIECELIN: Be patient, Sire. Don't die yet. When good weather returns, you will be well again.

NOBLE: I shall not last that long, my friends. My kingdom! Who will save my kingdom?

BRUN and YSENGRIN: *(At the same time.)* I! Me!

TIECELIN: Gentlemen.

YSENGRIN: *(Pushing Brun back.)* I can take your place, Sire. Don't be afraid to die.

BRUN: *(Elbowing Ysengrin away.)* I can do it, Sire. You may trust me.

TIECELIN: Don't die, your Majesty, or these two will kill each other to take possession of your throne.

NOBLE: Death is inexorable, my friends. There is only one who can help your poor, unfortunate King, and he is not here.

(Outbreak of savage barking.)

Listen!

BRUN: It is the dogs!

YSENGRIN: The dogs have broken through!

TIECELIN: The hunters have found us!

BRUN: They are coming!

YSENGRIN: We are trapped!

NOBLE: *(Struggling weakly to his feet.)* My friends, gather round me. We shall die together.

(*Cowering together in a close huddle, they await the enemy's approach. Lendore enters, followed by Reynard, disguised as a Minstrel.*)

LENDORE: Your Majesty —

NOBLE: Lendore!

TIECELIN: Lendore? It is not the hunters?

LENDORE: Hunters? It is only a poor Minstrel I found hiding beneath the barricade, to escape the dogs. I thought he might be able to help you.

BRUN: If he led the dogs to our stronghold, we are all done for.

TIECELIN: How did you get by the hunters?

REYNARD: *(Minstrel accent.)* Perdone, Senor. I no understanda very well.

YSENGRIN: Who are you, who plays the guitar while our King is dying?

BRUN: Cease your music, vagrant.

REYNARD: No de musique? Porque?

TIECELIN: The King is dying.

NOBLE: Let him approach. Who are you?

REYNARD: Un troubadour, from Andalusia d'Espagne, my gran Senor.

NOBLE: Can you play and sing?

REYNARD: Si. Very good player and singer. And very good doctor, too.

NOBLE: What? You are a doctor? Can you cure my pneumonia?

REYNARD: Si, Senor. I can cure anychosa.

BRUN: Beware. He is a spy.

REYNARD: I can save el gran Senor.

YSENGRIN: Get away.

REYNARD: I can kill la pneumonia, just like that — crac!

NOBLE: Do you really have a remedy?

REYNARD: Si, Senor, un gran remedia.

NOBLE: Relieve me of this cough, and you shall become my prime minister.

BRUN: Allow me, Sire —

NOBLE: I have spoken.

YSENGRIN: But your Majesty —

NOBLE: What remedy do you recommend?

REYNARD: *(Showing a bottle.)* Esta boteilla, gran Senor. Vino. Good vino. Vino grandissimo to kill la pneumonia.

NOBLE: Give it to me.

REYNARD: Ma, que, but it is not enough by itself. Needa still some otrechosa.

NOBLE: Some other things, such as what?

REYNARD: *(Makes gesture of pulling his moustache.)* Some chosa like this, but bigger, moocha bigger.

NOBLE: A big moustache?

REYNARD: Moustachio, si, yes. Yes, moustachio! Like that!
(Points to Brun.)

BRUN: My moustache?

REYNARD: Si, Senor. Si. Gracias.

NOBLE: Has it got to be cut?

REYNARD: Cut? Si, yes. That is of the most importance. It goes in la pocha —

(Shows his leather pouch.)

— and then on la cabeza, there.

(Indicates the King's head.)

NOBLE: Brun, your moustache.

BRUN: But Sire, it is impossible.

NOBLE: *(Stern.)* Your moustache.

BRUN: I shall be disgraced.

NOBLE: It is your King's life.

YSENGRIN: You cannot refuse, my dear Brun.

REYNARD: *(Scissors ready.)* Cut?

BRUN: Sire?

NOBLE: I am waiting.

YSENGRIN: Go ahead, troubadour.

(Reynard cuts off half of Brun's moustache.)

BRUN: Let Heaven be the witness of my disgrace!

NOBLE: It is for your King's welfare, Seigneur Brun.

REYNARD: It is truly un gran moustachio, Senor the Majesty. Half will be enough. No cut la otre. No wish to rob the fat senor.

BRUN: But Sire, I look ridiculous.

NOBLE: You will wear the half-moustache in remembrance of your self-sacrifice.

REYNARD: *(Putting moustache in his pouch.)* Ah, that is good, so far. But gran senor, that is not all.

NOBLE: You need something else? What is it?

REYNARD: A ball of white fur.

NOBLE: White fur?

REYNARD: Si. Oh, a very little ball. Perhaps no more than that.

(Points to Ysengrin's ears, which are lined with white.)

YSENGRIN: My ears? Oh, no!

(Frantically seeks a means of escape.)

REYNARD: Not the ears, senor. Only the white lining of them.

NOBLE: How lucky! Use your scissors, troubadour.

YSENGRIN: But Sire, I need my ear-linings!

BRUN: You cannot refuse, my dear Ysengrin.

NOBLE: This is for your King.

YSENGRIN: I shall never be the same!

NOBLE: Go ahead, Minstrel.

YSENGRIN: My ears! My ears!

REYNARD: *(Cutting.)* If the senor would only stand still — I do not wish to hurt the senor.

YSENGRIN: Ouch! He is taking my whole ear, Sire! Tell him to — Ouch!

REYNARD: Ah! Since the senor is so unhappy to lose a little bit of fur, we may content ourselves with this one piece.

(The ear he has trimmed has lost its erectness, hangs down ludicrously over one eye. The other ear stands up.)

YSENGRIN: But my ears will not match!

REYNARD: Small matter. We do not wish to ask too great a sacrifice of the senor.

YSENGRIN: I am lop-sided!

NOBLE: In the service of your King, Seigneur Wolf. You are sure you have enough white fur for the remedy, troubadour?

REYNARD: Oh, si, gran senor.

NOBLE: And now do you need anything else?

REYNARD: Only one otrechosa, Sire.

NOBLE: And what is that?

REYNARD: We must have three black feathers.

(Tiecelin starts creeping out.)

NOBLE: Tiecelin!

TIECELIN: You c-c-called me, Sire?

REYNARD: Ma, que, such beautiful, glossy black feathers!

NOBLE: Tiecelin, we have need of some feathers.

TIECELIN: But I have no feathers to spare, Sire.

REYNARD: Ah, si, si. On this side, too short. In front, too soft. On this side, the colour is not true. But ah, the back is just right.

(He seizes Tiecelin by the tail feathers.)

TIECELIN: Sire! He would not take my tail!

NOBLE: Do you find there what you require, troubadour?

REYNARD: Ah, si, si, Senor the Majesty.

TIECELIN: Help! Help! My beautiful tail!

YSENGRIN: Your tail is no better than my ear, Tiecelin.

BRUN: Or than my moustache.

REYNARD: *(Plucking.)* One!

TIECELIN: Aie!

NOBLE: It is for your King's life, Tiecelin.

REYNARD: Two!

TIECELIN: Aie!

YSENGRIN: At least you will not be one-sided.

REYNARD: Three!

TIECELIN: Aie! Oh, I am undressed! Sire, I shall take my death of cold.

(He does indeed look odd, with his stub tail.)

REYNARD: *(Placing feathers in the pouch.)* I regret any inconvenience this may cause the little senor. Now, your Majesty, all is ready. Gran senor. On la cabeza. There.

(He places the pouch inside Noble's crown.)

NOBLE: Are you sure this will cure me?

REYNARD: Oh, very sure, gran senor.

NOBLE: And if your remedy doesn't work?

REYNARD: Then we shall have to resort to extreme measures. But let us hope for the best.

NOBLE: No extreme measures. This will cure me. I can feel it. Give me that bottle.

REYNARD: Ah, si. This is the wine that gives life.

NOBLE: The moustache, what is it for?

REYNARD: Strength. It is the strength of the fat senor.

NOBLE: And the fur?

REYNARD: Warmth. It will dissolve the cough.

NOBLE: And the feathers?

REYNARD: It is a cover, to hold the strength and the warmth in. With the wine, it will spread through the body, and give new life. Drink.

(*Noble drinks. All watch with suspense.*)

TIECELIN: How does your Majesty feel?

NOBLE: To tell the truth, I don't feel any difference.

REYNARD: Ah, then, we shall have to use the last resort. For this I shall need three needles.

NOBLE: (*Alarmed.*) Needles? What for?

YSENGRIN: Needles? The Reverend!

BRUN: Of course. Epinard!

TIECELIN: I'll fetch him.

(*Exit.*)

NOBLE: What are these needles for?

REYNARD: Ah, Senor the Majesty is so very fortunate, to have such willing subjects to supply every need.

NOBLE: But what do you propose to do with these needles?

(*Tiecelin returns with Epinard.*)

TIECELIN: Master Troubadour, I have the honour to present the Reverend Epinard.

EPINARD: Peace be with you, Master Troubadour.

REYNARD: Ah, si. I can see that he has needles to spare.

EPINARD: (*Bristling.*) Needles? What is this about needles?

NOBLE: That is what I want to know.

REYNARD: We wish to request a small favour of you, Reverend, with your permission.

YSENGRIN: With or without your permission, his Majesty desires you to give up three needles to this troubadour here.

EPINARD: But my needles are my protection!

BRUN: Don't be stingy. You have plenty of them.

(Reynard has circled him, and selected three choice needles, between his ears.)

EPINARD: But your Majesty, I am not — Ow! Have some respect for my — Ow! Will you give me a chance to — Ow! Oh, I am unfrocked!

TIECELIN: It is for your King, Reverend.

REYNARD: Here are three needles, gran senor — nice and long and sharp.

NOBLE: Wait! I demand to know what you intend to do with these needles.

REYNARD: Why, if the first remedia has not cured you, it will be necessary to bleed you, Senor the Majesty.

NOBLE: Oh, no!

REYNARD: First in the arm —

NOBLE: Wait!

REYNARD: Then in the leg —

NOBLE: Stop!

REYNARD: And then, of course, in the — ah — underneath the — ah —

NOBLE: Enough! It is not necessary. I feel better now.

REYNARD: Ah, the remedia is taking effect?

NOBLE: I feel perfectly well. Throw those needles away.

REYNARD: My congratulations, Sire. The King is saved, gentlemen.

ALL: Long live the King!

NOBLE: Thank you. As for you, troubadour, I wish to reward you.

YSENGRIN: Are you going to make him your prime minister?

NOBLE: Did I say that?

BRUN: It is impossible, Sire. A Minstrel — a guitar-player —

NOBLE: Did I really promise it?

TIECELIN: According to law, Sire, a stranger cannot hold office in the animal kingdom.

NOBLE: Ah! You hear, Troubadour. The law prevents it.

REYNARD: The gran senor is cured, that is good. The povre Minstrel is not minister, that is also good. I ask only the gift of your royal favour in the country of los animalos.

NOBLE: Granted. Take this.

YSENGRIN: Your ring, Sire!

BRUN: The King's diamond!

TIECELIN: It is worth a million at least.

NOBLE: Is this too high a price for my life?

TIECELIN: No, indeed, indeed.

NOBLE: This ring will be the token of my royal protection. Whenever you show it to anyone in my kingdom, help and assistance will be granted you.

REYNARD: The senor is gran, gran como la luna. I am his servitor.

NOBLE: Do you wish anything else?

REYNARD: Only la pocha, there.

BRUN: My moustache!

NOBLE: Half of your moustache.

YSENGRIN: My ear!

NOBLE: The lining of one ear.

TIECELIN: My tail!

NOBLE: Three paltry feathers.

EPINARD: *(As Reynard tucks his quills into the pouch.)* **My** quills!

NOBLE: We wish you good luck, Minstrel.

REYNARD: Gracias, Senor the Majesty. Now I must go.

BRUN: Go? Out there?

TIECELIN: Sire, if he so much as snaps a twig going through the barricade, the dogs will be upon us in a flash.

REYNARD: Ma, que, Senors, the dogs will be upon me, not you. But have no fear, Majesty. I know how to escape the dogs.

NOBLE: Just the same, it would seem only wise for us all to take cover, until you are safely away. Follow me, gentlemen. Good bye, my good fellow.

REYNARD: The gran senor is good also. Viva, olle the gran senor. And gracias for the so beautiful ring.

(Noble exits, followed by Brun, Ysengrin, and Epinard. Tiecelin pretends to follow, but lags behind, as Reynard prepares to leave. Lendore has fallen asleep.)

TIECELIN: One moment, my friend.

REYNARD: The little senor said "my friend".

TIECELIN: I said "One moment". It is customary, in cases of audience with the King, to leave an expression of your thanks with me.

REYNARD: Ma, que, I did not know.

TIECELIN: Doubtless you do not know that I am the King's Registrar, and that I regulate, manage, and organize everything in the animal kingdom.

REYNARD: Hombre, que I, I thought the gran senor King did it all.

TIECELIN: He does what I command. When I say "Here comes the King", he comes. I say "The King sits down". He sits down. "The King drinks". He drinks. "The King gets up". He gets up. He can do nothing without my order. Without me there would be no King of the animals any more.

REYNARD: Ma, que, how about that! The little senor is a very important persona. It is a pity that he had to sacrifice his so beautiful tail plumage to the King's health.

TIECELIN: It is nothing less than a disgrace.

REYNARD: Ah, yes. Your costume is now a little lacking in dignity for a so important persona. Wait! I have a chosa in la pocha, to make him look more gran. Look. Would the senor do me the great honour to accept this, in place of the feathers he has lost?

(He takes out three peacock feathers.)

TIECELIN: They are peacock feathers, aren't they?

REYNARD: Si. The feathers del peacock. The very marvelosa bird que outshines the sun a hundred times, in his brilliance.

TIECELIN: He is a very beautiful bird indeed, but he is stupid.

REYNARD: Ma, que, but this is the tail, not the head. The little senor with the plumage del peacock, and his own gran intelligencio, will make the greatest bird of all, the very gran Phoenix of the occupantos of these woods.

TIECELIN: Do you think so?

REYNARD: Que, it is the truth. It is the thanks del troubadour to the gran persona del little senor.

TIECELIN: I accept the very humble present you give me. Now you may go.

REYNARD: Ah, si. Adios, senor.

TIECELIN: Take care, as you leave, not to draw the attention of the dogs.

REYNARD: Trust me, senor. Servitor, gran Phoenix. Servitor.

(Pretends to leave, but conceals himself on one side. Lendore stirs on the other side.)

TIECELIN: *(Listens tensely a few moments, for any possible disturbance caused by Minstrel's departure.)* Ah, he is safely away.

(Not noticing Lendore, he adorns himself with the peacock feathers.)

I can feel myself becoming very beautiful, very beautiful indeed. The King is far behind me when it comes to grace, charm, bearing, and elegance. I am really a Phoenix. The Minstrel said so. When the others see me, they will say "Look at the Crow!" And they will be green with envy. They will say "Look at the Crow!" And the echoes of the forest will endlessly repeat — "Look at the Crow!" Look at the Crow!"

REYNARD: *(Echoing.)* Oh! . . . Oh! . . . Oh! . . . Oh!

TIECELIN: How beautiful, beautiful, beautiful! How very beautiful! More beautiful than the Wolf, more beautiful even than the Lion.

(Shouts.) More beautiful than the King!

REYNARD: *(Echoing.)* . . . Ing! . . . Ing! . . . Ing! . . . Hee — hee — hee!

(Lendore takes it up, and the echo gradually changes into a laughter which is curiously prolonged.)

LENDORE: Hee — hee — hee — Hi — hi — hi —

TIECELIN: *(At first taken aback, stops and wonders.)* What? Hush, Echo.

REYNARD: Ho — ho — ho — ho —

LENDORE: Ho — ho — ho — ho —

TIECELIN: Instead of laughing, look at the Crow!

REYNARD: Ho — ho — ho — ho —

LENDORE: Ho — ho — ho — ho —

TIECELIN: *(In a rage.)* Are you almost through?

REYNARD: Hou — hou — hou — hou —

LENDORE: Hoo — hoo — hoo — hoo —

TIECELIN: You laugh at me?

REYNARD and LENDORE: Hee — hee — hee — hee —

(The laughter seems to come from everywhere at once.)

Ha — ha — ha — ha! Hee — hee — hee — hee! Look at the Crow! Ho — ho — ho! How beautiful is he! Hee — hee — hee! Ho — ho — ho! Ha — ha — ha! Hohoho! Hahaha! Hihihi! Hohohohahahahihi! Hohohohahahahihi!

(In shame Tiecelin divests himself of the peacock feathers, but the laughter continues to grow in volume.)

TIECELIN: *(Finally manages to top the laughter.)* Enough! Stop!

(Reynard stops, but Lendore, unaware of danger, continues, convulsed with genuine laughter.)

There is more to this than echoes.

(Creeping quietly across he discovers and seizes Lendore.)

Lendore! You were making fun of me!

LENDORE: I — I — Oh, Tiecelin, you were oh, so funny!

TIECELIN: Nobody is going to laugh at me, and live to tell it.

LENDORE: H — H — H — Stop! You are strangling me.

TIECELIN: *(Choking her.)* I am going to do more than that. I am going to feed you to the Wolf!

LENDORE: *(Struggling in his grasp.)* H-h-help! H-h-h-help!
(Reynard steps out of hiding, discarding his cape.)

REYNARD: Let her go.

TIECELIN: *(Frozen.)* I have surely heard that voice before.

REYNARD: Ma, que, senor, your costume is a little lacking in dignity —

TIECELIN: *(Trying shamefully to cover up his stub tail.)* Reynard! It is you!

REYNARD: At your service, Tiecelin.

TIECELIN: You, the Minstrel! I might have known it.

REYNARD: *(Placing peacock feathers at his tail and mimicking Tiecelin.)*

Am I not beautiful? The most beautiful of all? Am I not the great Phoenix of the deep woods?

TIECELIN: You will pay for this. It is your last trick. Everybody! Come! It is Reynard! It is his twenty-fifth crime! Trumpets! Trumpets!

REYNARD: Am I not splendid? Am I not the best-looking, the most intelligent —

(Trumpets. At the sound, Reynard breaks off short.)

TIECELIN: Everybody come! It is Reynard! Trumpets!

(Reynard runs desperately in all directions, seeking an escape. Trumpets.)

Twenty-fifth crime! Trumpets!

(Trumpets.)

VOICES: *(Off.)* Reynard! Twenty-fifth crime!

(The Epilogue follows immediately, without break.)

End of Scene Four

EPILOGUE

TIECELIN: By order of the King, his Majesty Noble the Lion —

REYNARD: All right. I know what is coming next.

(He tries to leave at right, but encounters Noble, entering, and has to bow.)

Sire.

NOBLE: Reynard.

(Reynard tries to leave at left, but Brun and Ysengrin enter there.)

REYNARD: Uncle Brun. Cousin Ysengrin.

BRUN: The rope is still in place.

YSENGRIN: We have kept it waiting for you.

REYNARD: I am in no hurry.

NOBLE: This time, Reynard, you have put the noose around your own neck.

LENDORE: Why did you let yourself get caught? Oh, Reynard, I cannot watch this!

(Exit. Epinard enters.)

EPINARD: What brings on this new disturbance? Ah, it is you, Reynard. You must be out of your mind.

NOBLE: Gentlemen.

TIECELIN: The King is about to speak. Trumpets!

(Trumpets.)

NOBLE: We are now at the end of the year of mercy granted to Reynard the Fox. What are the grievances charged against him now?

TIECELIN: A book full, your Majesty. Twenty-five crimes.
(He reads.)

The Knight Reynard, called Reynard the redhair, is accused —

NOBLE: Never mind, Tiecelin. You have all witnessed Reynard's misdeeds. So you will judge if he deserves to hang, or if he should be granted mercy. How do you feel about it?

YSENGRIN: I demand his hanging.

BRUN: Hang him!

TIECELIN: He must hang!

EPINARD: May Heaven forgive me, let him hang.

NOBLE: You hear, Reynard?

REYNARD: Nevertheless, your Majesty, I have the right to present my defense, I presume?

YSENGRIN: There is no defense.

TIECELIN: He has committed twenty-five crimes.

NOBLE: Have you any defender?

REYNARD: Yes, your Majesty.

NOBLE: Who is it?

REYNARD: You yourself, Sire.

NOBLE: I?

REYNARD: Doesn't this ring remind you of anything? *(Minstrel accent.)* The gran senor has lost la pneumonia. El troubadour has cured the gran senor.

NOBLE: So, it was you?

REYNARD: It was me, Sire, at your service.

(All the animals cry out with rage.)

BRUN: He has cut off half my moustache!

YSENGRIN: My ear!

EPINARD: My quills!

TIECELIN: *(Writing furiously.)* My feathers! And all this is going in the book!

BRUN: The bumble-bees have stung me all over!

EPINARD: He made away with my ham!

NOBLE: An end to this! Stop! Enough! Silence!

TIECELIN: Let the King speak.

(But the silence is broken by the sound of a hunting-horn, offstage. Lendore flies in, frantic.)

LENDORE: The hunters! The hunters are coming!

*(The hunting horn is repeated from a different direction, and **again** from another. Everyone is electrified.)*

They are closing in, from all sides of the woods!

BRUN: This has happened once before.

YSENGRIN: Is this rascal going to escape us again?

TIECELIN: The rope is ready.

BRUN: Let's not wait any longer. Hang him!

(Genuine rifle shots offstage.)

EPINARD: This is no joke!

NOBLE: We are caught!

(All make a grand rush for the left. The fanfare breaks out on that side, with renewed vigor.)

Tiecelin, go and see what is going on.

TIECELIN: B-b-b-but —

NOBLE: Go and see, I tell you.

EPINARD: It is no use, Sire. We are surrounded.

LENDORE: *(At right.)* There are more than twenty.

YSENGRIN: *(At back.)* They are coming this way, too.

BRUN: *(At left.)* And this way.

NOBLE: This time, my friends, we shall not escape the men. Let each one of you show your courage, and defend your life at a high price.

TIECELIN: Sire, I wish you a very gallant death. As for me, I have wings. Allow me to make use of them.

(Exit. His flight is hailed by shouts and rifle shots.)

BRUN: There goes our brave Phoenix.

YSENGRIN: What shall we do with the prisoner?

NOBLE: We are all prisoners, Seigneur Ysengrin.

REYNARD: I can save you, Sire.

BRUN: Don't listen to him. He is only trying to escape.

NOBLE: How can you save us?

REYNARD: Don't move from here. Stay under cover. I will go out of the woods. The fortifications will hold them until I can get out.

YSENGRIN: You see, he is only trying to get away.

REYNARD: I will let the hunters see me, willingly, in the open. The dogs will jump for me, and follow my tracks, and the men will follow them. I will lead them out of the woods, to the other end of the plain.

NOBLE: You will lose your life doing that.

REYNARD: It is possible — but it will save yours.

NOBLE: Release him. May Heaven help you!

REYNARD: Farewell, Sire. Farewell, my friends.

(He takes time to choose his exit point with care, then leaps out, to be greeted by furious dog-barking, men's shouts, and rifle shots. Ballet-mime, as the animals left onstage follow the progress of the chase. The cries, the barks, the shots, and the horn-calls intermingle. Cries and yells, close by at first — "The fox! The fox! Loose the dogs! Shoot! Shoot!" By some means, possibly by amplifying, there should be a noticeable difference between the human voices and the animal voices. At first the animals huddle together, frozen with terror, silent, distressed,

listening intently. As the offstage sounds retreat, they relax enough to register their fear, stopping up their ears, covering their heads, running for shelter, cowering under rocks, bushes, stumps. Eventually the noises fade away in the distance, indicating that Reynard is leading the chase far away. They begin to express their relief, and then their absolute joy, as the hunt moves further away, leaping with elation, embracing each other, dancing in triumph.)

LENDORE: *(Hopping up and down.)* He has done it! He has done it!

(One last, distant, terribly final shot, then a distressing silence.)

Oh, no!

(All are suddenly sobered.)

BRUN: And so, Sire, this is the end of Reynard.

EPINARD: May Heaven welcome his soul.

YSENGRIN: And the hunters his skin.

LENDORE: *(Who has rushed to the overlook.)* He is nowhere in sight.

YSENGRIN: Of course not. The dogs have got him.

NOBLE: He could outrun the dogs.

BRUN: But not the bullets, Sire.

YSENGRIN: The hunters have saved us the trouble of hanging him.

(Tiecelin returns, very cocky and proud.)

BRUN: Ah! Now that the danger is over, our valiant Crow returns.

TIECELIN: Sire, you are saved.

NOBLE: Where do you come from?

TIECELIN: From a tree, Sire. When I left here, I risked thousands of rifle shots — and look. Not a scratch.

LENDORE: Have you seen Reynard?

TIECELIN: He is dead. I saw him fall, covered with blood, and crawl under a hazelnut bush.

LENDORE: No!

NOBLE: The brave fellow!

TIECELIN: The dogs will catch up with him shortly. But they will find him dead. So will the hunters. I am the only one who saw his end.

YSENGRIN: Oh, stop your bragging. Reynard is dead, and that is all that matters.

LENDORE: *(Weeping.)* Poor redhair!

BRUN: We finally got rid of him.

EPINARD: Since he is gone, let him rest in peace.

NOBLE: At least he died like a hero — not by hanging.

(Reynard staggers in, tattered, exhausted, faltering, exaggerating his condition dramatically.)

REYNARD: Sire, my King —

TIECELIN: *(Hastily scrambling up his tree.)* What! You are not dead?

REYNARD: I . . . fulfilled . . . my promise —

(He staggers.)

NOBLE: Yes, good fellow. You have our undying gratitude.

LENDORE: Are you wounded?

REYNARD: No, it is nothing . . . no, nothing —

(He collapses.)

LENDORE: Reynard!

EPINARD: This time, Sire, beyond any doubt, he is really gone.

YSENGRIN: So much the better.

TIECELIN: Beware. He has more than one trick up his sleeve.

BRUN: Oh, no. Look.

(He lifts one leg, which falls back limply.)

TIECELIN: He did that to me once before.

(But he ventures down from his perch, nevertheless.)

EPINARD: *(Lifts one arm, which falls back, lifeless.)* He has undoubtedly passed away.

YSENGRIN: *(Lifts the tail, which falls back, a dead weight.)* There is no doubt indeed.

LENDORE: *(Sobbing.)* He was so good.

EPINARD: He was a rogue.

LENDORE: So witty.

YSENGRIN: He was a scoundrel.

LENDORE: So clever.

BRUN: He was a villain.

LENDORE: So full of fun.

TIECELIN: He was a cheese robber!

EPINARD: A ham robber!

BRUN: A moustache robber!

YSENGRIN: An ear robber!

TIECELIN: A tail robber!

EPINARD: A quill robber!

TIECELIN: And it is all down in my book. See, my book? Here are all his crimes.

NOBLE: Yes — and here is he. We live, because of him. Give me your book, Tiecelin. Let the accusations against him be buried with Reynard.

(He tears out pages, letting them fall on Reynard.)

TIECELIN: My book! My book!

(Silence. Reynard stirs.)

REYNARD: What gentle winds have blown this soft covering over my poor body? Ah, it is my noble King.

(He gathers loose pages and tears them across.)

What a relief it is to know that your royal person is safe from the hunters!

(He rises.)

BRUN: He lives!

LENDORE: Reynard, my friend!

YSENGRIN: He is alive!

TIECELIN: My book! My book!

REYNARD: Ah, you are concerned about your book, Tiecelin? Allow me to return it to you — at least a part of it. And a part for you, Uncle Brun. And some for you, Ysengrin.

(Gaily he pelts them all with torn fragments. Tiecelin, driven to despair by this desecration, scrambles about frantically, trying to gather them up.)

BRUN: Sire, he lives — and there goes all the evidence against him.

REYNARD: Indeed. Then we shall have no use for this grim thing. Let us use it for a gayer purpose.

(He snatches down the hanging-rope, jumps rope for a few steps.)

Come, my faithful friend Lendore, it is a moment to rejoice. If you will hold this end, perhaps the Reverend will be good enough to hold the other?

TIECELIN: *(Picking up torn pages.)* My book! My book!

YSENGRIN: Sire, he is free to start his crimes all over again.

NOBLE: Reynard, you are really a very bad fellow.

REYNARD: I know, Sire. We all have a little bad in us, don't we? Reverend, can't you turn a little faster?

EPINARD: Reynard, you have not changed one bit.

REYNARD: Faster, Lendore. Sire, won't you join me?

(He takes Noble's hand, and leads him into the game.)

LENDORE: Reynard is alive!

(And as the rope twirls faster, all take up the refrain.)

BRUN: *(Grumpy.)* Reynard is alive.

YSENGRIN: *(Bitter.)* Reynard is alive.

EPINARD: *(Resigned.)* Reynard is alive.

TIECELIN: *(In tears with frustration.)* My book! My book!

NOBLE: *(Amused.)* Reynard is alive!

LENDORE: *(Joyful.)* Reynard is alive!

REYNARD: *(Triumphant.)* Reynard is alive!

The End

FROM THE DESK OF

DOMI SCHIRO

COSTUME—MAKE-UP DESIGNS

By
Irene Corey

COSTUME-MAKE-UP DESIGNS

for

REYNARD THE FOX

by IRENE COREY

The costume and make-up designs for this play are intended as a definite theatrical policy: costume and make-up are inseparable, and should be planned as a unit. This is not a new theory, as it has been practiced for centuries in the Oriental theatre. My experience is that this principle works effectively on stage, giving a force and unity which strengthens and underlines the actor's characterization.

The style of make-up devised for the purpose of REYNARD THE FOX is applied directly to the actor's face, resulting in a make-up mask, rather than a papier-mache mask. Since the make-up mask preserves the expressiveness of the actor's face, and also leaves the mouth free for voice projection, it offers obvious advantages for the play's characters, so the make-up is treated here in detail. It is essential to the effectiveness of the make-up mask that the colour of the skin exactly match the colour of the wimple, where they are juxtaposed. This makes the mask and costume one unit, which is the underlying philosophy of this approach. The make-up plans are superimposed over a basic face drawing. The natural human features serve as landmarks only, since the regular features are to be ignored in favour of the designed areas. Thus a mouth or a nose may move inches away from its normal habitat. The letters are numbered in sequence, according to reference in the instructions. It is not easy, but a mature person can do it in less time than it takes papier-mache to dry — and it is rewarding to start with a normal face, and end up with a lion!

It has been my experience that stick grease-paint has the best consistency for the make-up mask. Tube grease-paint is oily, and tends to blot up too much powder, which cuts down the intensity of the colours. The shades of the colours may need to be darkened, or intensified, for large auditoriums, or under heavy lighting conditions. The brush preferred is a flat, square-¼-inch sable brush. Caution must be taken to distinguish between the numbers indicated for *Base* colours, and for *Lining* colours, as they have a separate series. (The make-up numbers used in the accompanying instructions refer to Stein's make-up, but their equivalent may be found in make-up supplied by other houses.)

As to costumes, the yardages are not indicated, since the size of the performer is not known. For gluing fabrics, satisfactory results may be obtained with "Elmer's" or "Sobo", a white liquid which comes in squeeze bottles, and dries clear. Gluing eliminates turning under raw edges, and costumes can then be dry-cleaned, but not washed.

If the fabrics or leotards cannot be obtained in the colours wanted, dye them. Automatic washers have taken the pain out of dyeing, and will distribute the colour evenly. Good effects can be achieved by "over-dyeing". For instance, if the colour wanted is yellow-brown, buy brown tights, and put them in a gold dye-bath.

I hope that the instructions for costume and make-up will be clear, even to the novice — and that for the more experienced, the instructions will serve only as a spring-board for his own imagination.

REYNARD, THE FOX

FOX COSTUME PROCEDURE

Materials:
    Leotards and T-Shirt: orange.
    Socks: black stretch.
    Mittens: black.
    "Fur" material: orange, white, black, and grey organdy.
    Ear Linings: white organdy.
    Mitten cuffs: black cotton and interlining.
    Tunic: emerald green Indian Head.
    Tunic Trim: red satin, white cotton broadcloth.
    Minstrel Disguise Cape: red felt, or red broadcloth lined with black broadcloth.
    Cape Trim: yellow balls from balled fringe used on draperies.
    Pouch: gold felt, or cotton broadcloth, interlined.
    Belt: black.

Desired Effect: The slender arms and legs should contrast with the saucy head and tail. The flowing lines of the tunic decor contribute to the svelte appearance of proud and crafty Reynard. The bold contrast of red and green complement his strong ego.

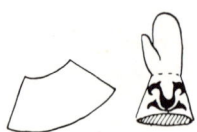

1. *Basic Garments:*
   To keep the sleeves of the T-shirt taut, tack the mittens to them. Make trial paper pattern for cuffs from semi-circle. Cut from black material and interline. Attach to mittens. Cut design from red satin, and glue to cuff.

   Put black stretch socks over leotards, and roll tops down.

2. *Wimple:*
   Cut from orange organdy. See *Wolf* for directions.

3. *Ears:*
   See *Wolf* for directions, but cut from orange and white organdy. Semi-circle will be 5½ inches in diameter. Sew the white organdy tufts in.

4. *Fur:*

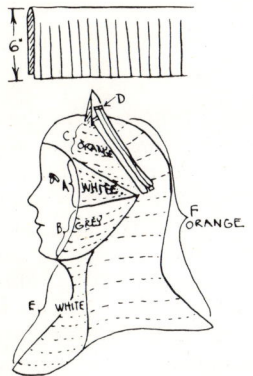

Cut white organdy into 12x36 inch strips. Fold, and cut raw edges into ¾ inch strips.

Area A: Sew fringe on lines, starting at the bottom and working to the top. The folded seam edge will point toward the top of the head.

Area B: Cut 12 inch fringe from grey organdy, and treat the same as white. Stitch to Area B, starting on the top line, with the folded seam edge pointing down. Proceed to the bottom of the area.

Area C: Cut orange organdy the same as white and grey. Sew on Area C, starting with the lowest line, and proceeding upward.

Area D: Stitch two short rows of orange organdy, 12 inches long, to the back of each ear.

Looking at the head from the front, pull all of the tufts to a point at the side. Trim the ends to achieve the pointed effect, if necessary. Lightly baste the ends to a point, not drawing the thread tight.

Area E: Cut white organdy in strips 4 inches wide. Fold and fringe into ½ inch strips, from the raw edges. Sew these fringes on lines indicated in Area E, working from bottom to the top. Each row should slightly overlap.

Area F: Cut orange organdy the same as for Area E. Sew to lines in Area F, covering the rest of the wimple. Start at the bottom line and work up, making each row slightly overlap.

Upper Arms: Sew a few rows of orange organdy fringe on the upper arm of T-Shirt to give a sense of continuation from the head-piece.

5. *Tunic:*

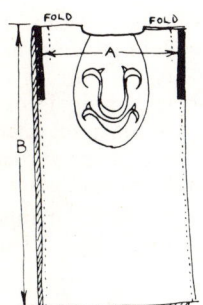

Lay emerald green material on a fold.
Measurements:

A. Across the shoulders, plus 8 inches.

B. Shoulder to above knee.

Leave shoulders on the fold and cut an oval neck, large enough to go over the head.

Sew side seams up to armhole openings. Hem.

Glue white cotton oval to chest area. Cut design from red satin and glue in place, (or sew).

On back of tunic locate Tail exit, and glue a red satin design similar to the one in front. Take 2 inch pleats on shoulders of tunic. Fasten with black belt.

6. *Tail:*

TAIL EXIT DESIGN

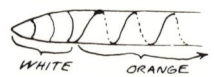

WHITE ORANGE

Construct the basic tail the same as the *Lion*, using orange organdy, and making it floor length, plus a few inches to trail. Make orange organdy fringe as for headpiece, measuring 8 inches wide when folded, and cut into ¾ inch strips. Sew around the tail in a continuous spiral. At the very tip, substitute white organdy. A black effect down the top of the tail could be achieved by spraying black spray dye quickly down the center. Using the same spray dye (available in connection with dyeing furniture and rugs), spray the leotards around the ankles, fading upward toward the calf, and around the wrist away from the cuff toward the elbow.

7. *Minstrel Disguise, Cape:*

Measurements:

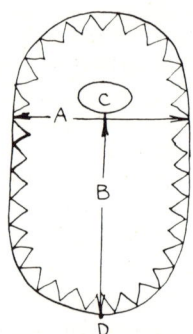

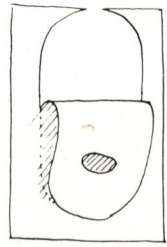

A. Run a tape from the elbow up the arm, across the shoulder and down to the other elbow. The center of this line forms the radius point for the upper part of the oval.

B. From neck to knees.

C. Measure around headpiece to determine how large the neck of the cape should be to allow it to slip on over.

When top of oval is cut out, fold it over to the mark showing length to knees, (D) and draw off the lower part of the oval. Connect with straight lines.

The easiest fabric to make this cape from is red felt because it will necessitate no hemming, after the edges are cut into zig-zags. If red broadcloth with black lining is used, cut double, turn right sides together, mark zig-zags with chalk, and sew. Turn through the neck, after clipping and trimming seams.

Sew on yellow balls from balled fringe, substituting two or three jingle bells, if desired.

8. *Hood:*

   Measurements:

   A. Approximately 14 inches.

   B. Approximately 18 inches, or from center of the top of the head around the side tufts, under the chin. It should not be too tight.

   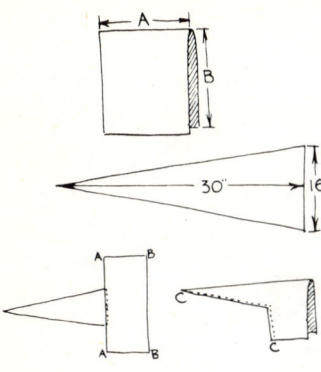

   Cut a triangular piece 16x30 inches. Open the hood piece and sew the back of it to the end of the triangle. Crease along the fold line, joining A's and B's and stitch line C.

   Sew into the neck of the cape, taking tucks in the hood to make it fit. If using red broadcloth instead of felt, line with black. Sew a ball to the tip of the point.

9. *Pouch:*

   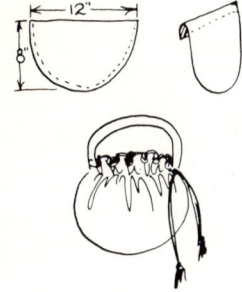

   Material: Gold felt, or gold cotton, interlined.

   Cut according to the measurements given in the diagram. Stitch together around curved edge. Turn. Turn under 1 inch along top edge. Insert shoe string with tasseled end. Sew on handle, made of a strip of felt 2½ inches wide; double and then stitch edges. Run the belt through the handle.

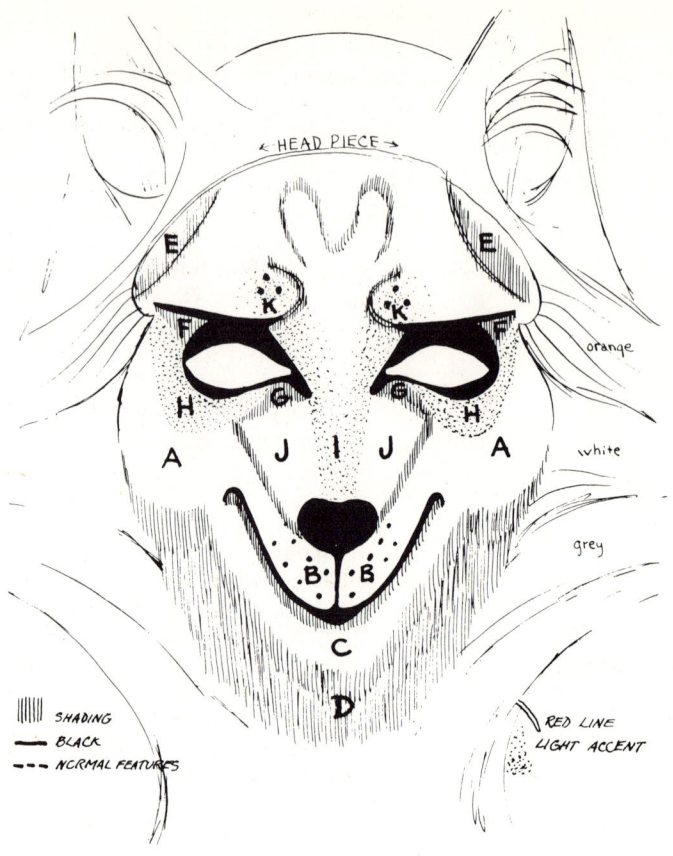

MAKEUP SUPPLIES: *

    Base: Upper Half, #8 Dark Sunburn Base, (or mix to match the shade of orange organdy used in costume).

             Middle Half, #22 White Base.

             Lower Half, #4 Grey Base.

    Shadow: #25 Red-Brown Liner, and #4 Grey Liner.

    Light Accent: #8 Dark Sunburn, lightened with White and Yellow, and tinted with a little #2 Moist Rouge.

    Eyes, Nose, Mouth: #25 Black Base.

    Accent: #2 Medium Red Moist Rouge.

* *All make-up numbers refer to Stein's grease stick make-up. If other make-up is preferred, please consult their charts to co-relate colours.*

FOX MAKEUP PROCEDURE

1. Apply a small amount of cold cream, and remove with tissues.
2. With #22 White Base draw in temple lines and the line which shapes the cheeks and pointed chin. Apply white base to the area occupied by the cheekbones, chops, and false chin, (Areas A, B, C.) Add #4 Grey Base from the cheek and chin line down, all the way to the wimple, (Area D), matching the grey of the headpiece.
3. The upper half of the face is covered with a base of #8 Dark Sunburn, extending from the forehead down through Area H, under the eyes, and Areas I and J of the nose. It should blend with the orange of the costume.
4. Using #25 Red-Brown Liner, draw in all features: eyes, frown and worry lines, mouth and nose. Soften the edges of these lines. Create shadows in the temples, (Areas E), under the false eyebrow, (Areas F), and the eye bag, (Areas G), and along the side nose lines.
5. Make a shadow along the mouth line, with #4 Grey Liner.
6. With #25 Black Base, fill in the eyes, nose and mouth, as shown. The nose should start up above the tip of the natural nose, extending no wider than necessary to include the nostril opening. The pointed effect of the mouth is painted on the bottom lip.
7. The light color accent is made by mixing #8 Dark Sunburn base with White and Yellow, with just a dab of medium red rouge. This mixture is applied to the following areas:

    Area H, under eye: Fill in solidly, slightly fusing along the edge next to the white cheekbone.

    Area I, center of nose: Apply solidly from nose up to the bottom of eyes, then fade out in the center, keeping solid next to the slanting eye lines.

    Areas K, frown puffs: Start in the center of the puffs, and fade edges.
8. Draw a red line around the mouth, underneath the black line.
9. Add round dots for whiskers and chops, and frown puffs.
10. If actual whiskers are desired, see instructions for the *Bear*.

YSENGRIN, THE WOLF

WOLF COSTUME PROCEDURE

Materials:

Leotards and long-sleeved T-Shirt: yellow-brown.
Mittens: yellow-brown.
Socks: yellow-brown.
"Fur" material: any soft, "floppy" material, preferably outing flannel, in yellow-brown.
Ear linings: white organdy and white broadcloth.
Tunic and cape: lime green and bright yellow in Indian Head, or cotton broadcloth.
Trim: red satin, red bias tape (or satin ribbon).
Claws: felt and glue.
Belt: brown.

Desired Effect: The yellowish tones of Monsieur Ysegrin's costume are chosen to relate to his cowardly streak. The raggedy outline achieved by his fur and crenellated cape contribute to his unkempt look. The accents of red reveal his capability for devilment, particularly in the realm of chickens, where his prize trophy is the chicken feather.

1. *Basic garments:*

    The mittens are sewed to the ends of the T-Shirt sleeves. Wear the socks over the leotards, rolling the tops down. Mark toes on mittens and socks with ink marker. Glue on felt pads, and attach claws as for the lion.

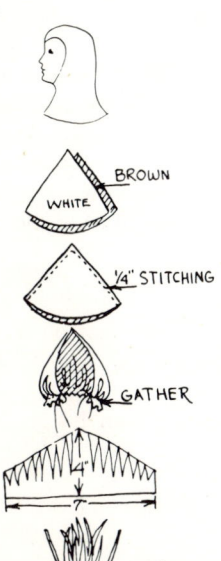

2. *Wimple:*

    Cut from brown flannel according to the directions given under *Lion*, only make the front dip down over the forehead, as shown in the makeup sketch. Make hooked opening under the chin, and eliminate the elastic.

3. *Ears:*

    Make a half circle which has a diameter of 9 inches, from flannel and another from white broadcloth. Cut each semi-circle in half, and placing a piece of each color together, sew the straight sides. Turn, and stitch ¼ inch from edge. Run a gathering thread along the curved edge, pulling it into a cupped shape. Tack ears to wimple.

Cut a single layer of white organdy into a triangle 7 inches at the base, 4 inches tall, and fringe from top downward. Draw together at the bottom with a piece of copper wire, leaving two ends sticking up which are the same height as the ear. Place in the ear by running ends of wire between the edge and the ¼ inch stitching. When one ear is "plucked" of its lining the wire comes out too, letting the ear fall.

4. *Fur:*

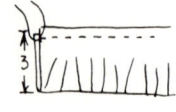

Cut brown flannel into strips 6 inches wide, which become 3 inches when folded. Cut strips up through the folded edge in irregular widths and lengths, but not cutting deeper than halfway. These fringes will be gathered along the raw edges to give bulk to the fur. Where more of a bunchy appearance is needed, such as on either side of the face, and at the back of the head, increase the gathering.

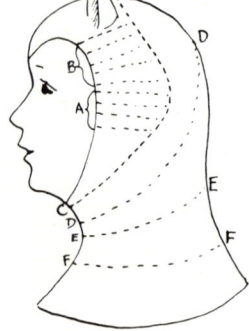

Area A: Stitch fringe to the wimple along the dotted lines. Note how the lengths of the dotted lines vary.

Area B: Fringe strips are 4 inches wide, folded.

Line C: Sew a fringe strip 5 inches wide, folded, all the way around the wimple.

Line D: Fringe strip 6 inches wide, folded.

Line E: Fringe strip 6 inches wide, starting immediately under Line D in front, and dropping to just under the loops of D in the back.

Line F: Same as E.

On top of the wimple, over the forehead stitch two rows of loops 1½ inches wide, folded, as shown in lines A and B.

5. *Elbow Tufts:*

Sew a few tufts of fringe at the back of the sleeve, at the elbow.

6. *Tail:*

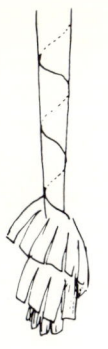

Make the basic tail the same as for the lion. The length should be about 18 inches long, or at least 6 inches shorter than the fox tail. Create the "bush" by sewing a continuous row of gathered fringe (6 inches wide, folded), around the tail. If you use the same brown outing used for the headpiece, it will make a shaggy, heavy tail. If a lighter effect is desired, use folded organdy.

Attach to the reinforced leotards, and make a "tail holster" as for the lion.

7. *Tunic:*

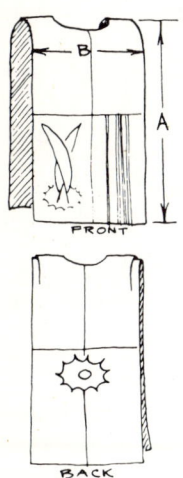

Measurements:

A. Shoulder to above knee.

B. Across shoulders plus 8 inches.

Fold yellow material, mark and cut. Cut oval neckline, large enough to go over head without an opening down back. Either line with yellow or lime, or hem edges. Find waistline and cut rectangle of lime to be stitched over half of skirt. Cut feathers out of the yellow material, and the oval splotch out of red satin. Glue in place. Also glue (or sew) red satin ribbon, (or red bias tape), on opposite side. Make 2 inch pleats over each shoulder.

Back: Determine where the tail will exit from the costume, and cut a hole. Around the hole, glue on the red satin design.

8. *Cape:*

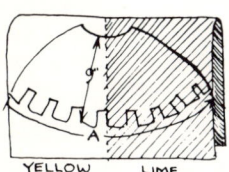

Measurements:

A. Around arms and chest, plus room for movement.

B. About 9 inches.

Sew lime and yellow material together, vertically. Fold. Draw cape pattern. Let the neck fit, with an opening at the back. Cut a second cape out of lime or yellow for lining. Put right sides together, sew side seams and crenellated edge. Turn, and bind neck. Trim with red stripes over the yellow side.

MAKEUP SUPPLIES: *

    Base: #7 Brown Liner mixed with #16 Yellow Liner.

    Eyes, nose, and mouth: #25 Black Base.

    Shadow: #25 Red-Brown Liner.

    Light accent areas: #16 Yellow Liner.

    Accent Color: #2 Medium Red Moist Rouge.

    Black Tooth Wax.

* *All make-up numbers refer to Stein's grease stick make-up. If other make-up is preferred, please consult their charts to co-relate colours.*

WOLF MAKEUP PROCEDURE

1. Draw in all lines with #7 Brown Liner. Inside the large area surrounding the eyes and nose, apply base made from #7 Brown Liner, mixed with #16 Yellow Liner, with the yellow tone predominant. On the surrounding face area, apply base made of the same colors with brown predominating. This color should match the color of the headpiece. Fuse the line where the two areas meet.

2. Apply #25 Black Base around the eyes as shown. To give the bridge of the nose a wider appearance, start at the corner of the natural eye. The whole eyelid will be black. The nose button begins on the under part of the natural nose, next to the nostrils, and extends underneath in the form of an oval. The cleft extends down to the lower part of the upper lip, and continues as the mouth line upward.

3. Apply Medium Red Moist Rouge as shadow under the eye, in the form of a bag, (Areas A). Apply, also, at the top corner of the false eye, (Areas B), fading at the lower edge. Make the false nose line (Areas C), fusing outside edges of line.

4. Using #16 Yellow Liner, accent the following areas:
   Area D, nose: Apply solidly next to black nose, fusing into red side nose lines. Carry up the nose solidly, against the slanted eye lines, fading out above eyes.
   Areas E, around the eyes: Fill in solidly against the black orb of the false eye, fusing into the red shadows and cheekbones.
   Areas F, the chops: Fill in solidly against the black mouth line and nose, fusing into red side nose lines. Accent laugh pouches at end of mouth.
   Area G, Lower Lip: Apply to center of area, and fade sides.

5. Shadow with #25 Red-Brown Liner around the mouth, under the main mouth line; along the line of chin whiskers, fading out toward outside of face; and above the nose at the dip in the forehead, fading up toward the wimple.

6. Brush in bold black lines representing fur around the chin, and eyes, as shown by the heavy black lines.

7. Using the red rouge, put on the final accents by drawing a red line under the black mouth line, and on the bag under the eyes.

8. Black out one front tooth with tooth wax.

BRUN, THE BEAR

BEAR COSTUME PROCEDURE

Materials:
  Leotards, and long-sleeved T-Shirt: dark red-brown.
  Mittens: dark red-brown.
  Stretch socks: dark red-brown.
  "Fur" material: red-brown organdy.
  Ear linings: black organdy.
  Tunic: white Indian Head or denim, with red broadcloth and white satin trim.
  Belt: brown.
  Paunch: pillow.

Desired Effect: The organdy will furnish the loops with the proper bounce to create a burly, bulky look, contrasting with the tiny hands and feet. The bear's sullen, bellicose humor is exemplified by the bumble-bee, whose fierce stripes typify that for which the bear has a healthy respect.

1. *Basic Garments:*

   Sew the mittens to the sleeves of the T-Shirt, which should be bought one or two sizes larger than the actor normally wears to allow room for the padding. Wear the socks over the feet of the leotards, but do not let roll show; hide it under the last row of fur. Glue black felt pads to mittens.

2. *Wimple:*

   Cut according to the variations given under *Wolf*, only shaping it with a dip in the forehead, as shown in the makeup drawing.

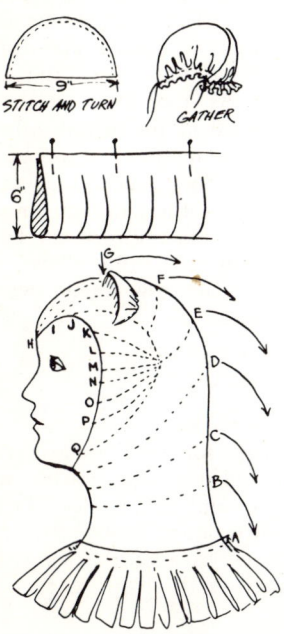

3. *Ears:*

   Cut two circles with a diameter of 9 inches; one dark brown, and one black. Cut in half. Treat the two semi-circles the same as the *Lion's* ear. Attach to the wimple.

4. *Fur:*

   Cut red-brown organdy into pieces 12x36 inches. Fold, but do not crease the folded edge. Pin raw edges together. Cut from the folded edge up, into strips 1 inch wide.

   Mark off lines on wimple as shown by dotted lines in illustration. Starting on the lowest dotted line, A, stitch raw edges of the fringe, proceeding upward through line G. For the top of the wimple, cut fringes which are 2 inches wide when folded. Sew on Lines H, I, J with raw seam edge pointing toward seam. Note extension of Line J, behind ear.

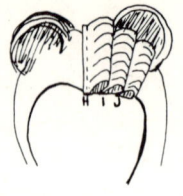

On Lines K, L, and M, the loops are 8½ inches long, folded, and are sewed on in the same direction as the preceding ones.

M is a 10 inch fringe, sewed the same way.

N is also 10 inches folded, but the raw seam edge is now pointed downward and sewed in place, forcing the loop upward in direction. O, P, and Q, are fringes 8½ inches wide, and are sewed with the raw edges facing down.

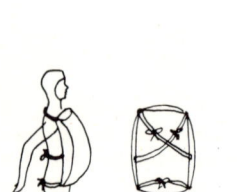

BACK OF PILLOW

5. *Paunch:*

Either make a paunch from muslin and cotton batting, or use a pillow. Sew ties at the top, bottom and sides. Tie in the back.

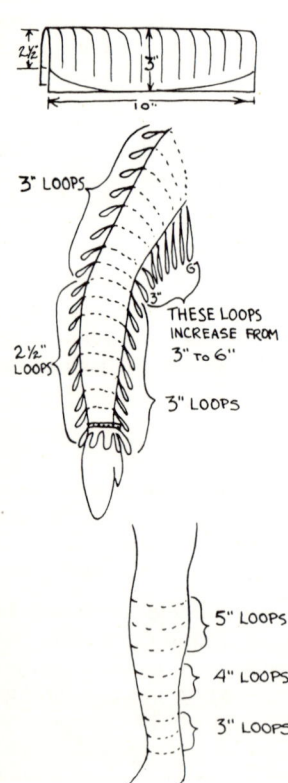

6. *Arms:*

Cut strips of red-brown organdy 6 inches wide, and 10 inches long, and fold. Cut raw edges in a curve, tapering from 2½ inches on the ends, to 3 inches in the middle. Run a gathering thread along the curved edge. Pull the fullness into the center of the fringe, leaving ends smooth. Sew the end of the fringe to the outside of the wrist, making the longest and fullest part of the fringe fall under the arm, creating bulk. As the rows of fringe progress up the arm, the length of the fringe pieces will increase to about 15 inches around the elbow, and 20 inches on the upper arm. See the diagram for suggested increase in the length of the loops, starting with 3 inches at the elbow, and increasing to 6. Each row should overlap the preceding one.

7. *Legs:*

The fringe strips for the legs are made from straight folded pieces, starting with 3 inch loops around the ankles, then 4 inch, and 5 inch loops around the calf. Extra bulk at the back of the leg is obtained by gathering the loops as they are sewed on.

8. *Tunic:*

Material: White Indian Head or **Denim**.

Measurements:

A. Distance across shoulders plus 8 inches.

B. Distance around stomach, measured over the paunch, plus 5 inches.

C. Distance from the shoulder to 10 inches from the floor.

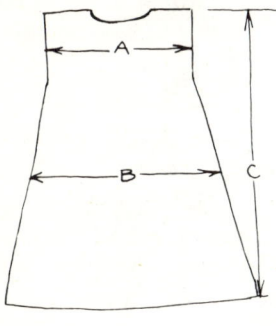

Cut neck in oval, large enough to go over head without an opening. Sew on dotted lines, leaving opening for arms.

Trim: Divide front (the back may be done, too, but it is optional), in half vertically, and horizontally along the line of the low-slung belt. Glue, or sew, wide (2 inch) stripes of red cotton to upper-left, and lower-right rectangles. Cut body and legs of Bumble bee from red cotton, and glue in place. Cut the white stripes and wings of the bee from white satin. Draw in outline with ink marker.

9. *Belt:*

Brown leather belt may be used, or it may be made of cloth, backed with heavy black belting.

MAKEUP SUPPLIES: *

    Base: Outer face: #8 Dark Sunburn Base, mixed with #25 Red-Brown Liner. (Or any colors necessary to match costume).
    Inner face: #8 Dark Sunburn Base, plus White.

    Shadow: #25 red-brown Liner.

    Light Accent: # Dark Sunburn, with White.

    Mouth, Nose and Eyes: #5 Black Base.

    Mouth Accent: #2 Moist Rouge, Medium Red.

* *All make-up numbers refer to Stein's grease stick make-up. If other make-up is preferred, please consult their charts to co-relate colours.*

BEAR MAKEUP PROCEDURE

1. Divide the face into two parts by drawing the area which goes around the eyes, chops and chin, with #8 Dark Sunburn Base.
2. Apply #8 mixed with White Base to the areas surrounding the eyes, nose, and mouth, (Areas A, B, C, and D.)
3. Make the remaining parts of the face, (Areas H and G), #8 Dark Sunburn slightly darkened with #25 Red-Brown Liner, mixed to match the color of the costume next to the face.
4. Draw in all lines with #25 Red-Brown Liner: Eyelids, (higher than normal lids), eye bag lines, chops, nose, and furrow between brows. Fuse the edges of all these lines except on the eyes and eyelids.
5. Mix the light accent color from Dark Sunburn and White, and apply to the following areas:
   Areas A, above eye: Accent center of area and fuse edges.
   Areas B, cheekbones: Accent along fur line, fading toward eye.
   Area C, nose: Fill in solidly next to button nose, fading as you go toward the sides and top.
   Areas D, chops: Solid against button nose and mouth line.
   Areas E, chin: Solid in center next to mouth, fading toward chin.
   Areas F, false eyelids: Fill in solidly from the lashes up to the line which has been drawn to indicate the top of the false eye lid. This will cover all of the normal eyelid.
6. Fill in with Black on the nose, mouth line, whisker dots, half moon under the eye, lines marking false eyelid, line along the upper lashes of the eye. Make definite brush strokes for fur around the chin, eyes, and furrowed brow.
7. Using White, make "fur" brush strokes between the black strokes, around the eyes, only.
8. Draw a red line under the black mouth line.
9. Powder.
10. Cut whiskers from black organdy, by pattern as shown, and glue on with spirit gum. Curl whiskers downward, over the fingers. The organdy will be opaque, and makeup may need strengthening over it, after the glue has dried.

TIECELIN, THE CROW

CROW COSTUME PROCEDURE

Materials:
  Leotards and long-sleeved T-shirt: black.
  Gloves: black tight-fitting nylon.
  Socks: yellow; one pair men's plastic working gloves, yellow.
  Feathers: black satin.
  Wings: black net.
  Tail feathers: black organdy, and wire; and spring paper clamp.
  Hat: red-orange organdy, or red-orange felt, optional satin lining; pin.
  Golden necklace.
  Padding: cotton batting, black broadcloth.

Desired Effect: Because Tiecelin is a crow, he must be black. The monotony of the over-all color is relieved by changing textures, with the shining satin breast feathers contrasting with the crisp net wings. His honorable position in the court is symbolized by the heavy gold chain. Since Tiecelin's ego can be bolstered by the addition of a peacock's feather to his tail, his hat choice woud lean toward the selection of a flambouyant comb effect.

1. *Basic Garments:*
   Either black leotards worn with a black T-shirt, or a one-piece pair of leotards, may be used. To keep the sleeve taut, the gloves should be sewed in.

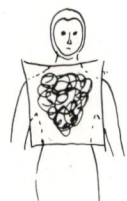

2. *Chest Padding:*
   Lay a piece of black cotton on the chest of the actor, over the T-shirt. Place cotton batting on top in layers, slowly forming the desired shape. Taper to normal chest level at the edges. Lay another piece of black material on top of the cotton, pinning in darts where necessary to conform to the shape of the cotton. Trim edges of both layers of fabric to the shape of the cotton.

Before sewing the top piece on, cover it with satin feathers (See instruction #5 for *Feathers* below.)

After the edges of the padding are hemmed, whip in place on to the T-shirt. Use loose stitches to allow for stretch when pulling T-shirt on. If too tight fitting for this, snap the padding in place after the shirt is on.

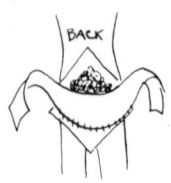

3. *Tail Padding:*

Cover the seat of the actor, (over the leotards) with a square of black cotton, with the bias running up and down. Stretch to fit over the hips. Build out the tail pad with cotton batting, as on the chest. Check with the costume sketch for the silhouette desired. Another bias strip should be pinned to the under part of the pad, forming a "sling" to hold the padding. Pull the bias strip over the cotton, tacking edges in place. Tack the whole thing to the leotards.

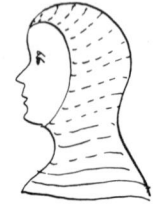

4. *Wimple:*

Cut wimple as for *Wolf*, from black cotton. There is a slight point over the forehead.

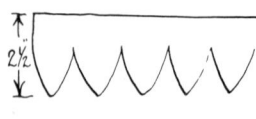

5. *Feathers:*

Cut black satin into strips $2\frac{1}{2}$ x 36 inches long. Scallop into feather shapes, up to $\frac{1}{2}$ inch from the top. Sew on the wimple in single thicknesses, starting at the bottom, and working to the top, until the entire wimple is covered. Allow each layer to overlap slightly.

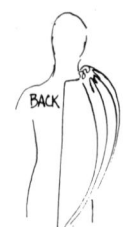

6. *Wings:*

Using black net, cut a width long enough to reach from under the neck in front of the shoulder in a loose drape, to the point of the tail. Start draping one side at center back, leaving it smooth, across the back, and gathering as you reach the shoulder and go over the arm around to side front. Place the wimple over this, and tack the net to the bottom edge of the wimple. Trim off excess net.

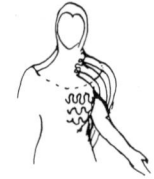

Pull the center back area taut to the tip of the tail, and loosely drape the gathered portion over the top of the arm, pulling it back to the tip of the tail. At the tail, loosely baste net together and then trim.

7. *Tail Feathers:*

Using wire which will hold its shape and not bend easily, glue it as the spine down the center of two layers of organdy cut in the shape of feathers. Make four feathers, measuring 10, 12, 14, and 17 inches long, and $2\frac{1}{2}$ inches wide. A 12 inch wire stub should be left on each wire, below the organdy. Sew one tail feather in place.

8. *Tail Feather Mounting:*

At the tip of the tail padding under the net tuft, sew securely one large paper spring clamp, which has been painted black. Clamp feathers in this, so they may be pulled out during the action of the play.

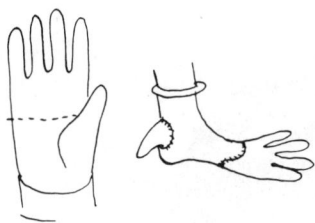

9. *Feet:*

Buy a pair of men's working gloves, in yellow plastic. Cut just above the thumb. Slip over the toe of the sock, pulling sides tight to spread fingers, which have now become toes. Sew thumb to back of sock for the spur.

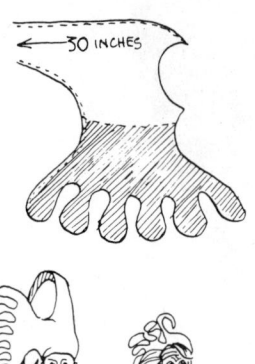

10. *Medieval Hat:*

On orange-red organdy, mark as for wimple, but make a tail which is at least 40 inches long. This may be pieced. Pink deep scallops in the shoulder edge. Sew on the dotted lines and turn. (Satin lining sewed from the chin down, would be very effective.) If felt is used, pinking and lining will be unnecessary.

Place on the head with the face opening going around the top of the head. Bring the tail under the scalloped part and wrap it around the head, tucking the end in. Fasten with a large gold costume pin. The scalloped edges will tumble and fall in a sort of "Cock's Comb".

11. *Official Necklace:*

This should be a very heavy gold chain, similar to costume jewelry belts, with a large round pendant in center front. The chain can be made from cross sections sawed from black walnuts, painted gold, and strung on gold ribbon. Or they may be cut from felt and treated like the lion's claws.

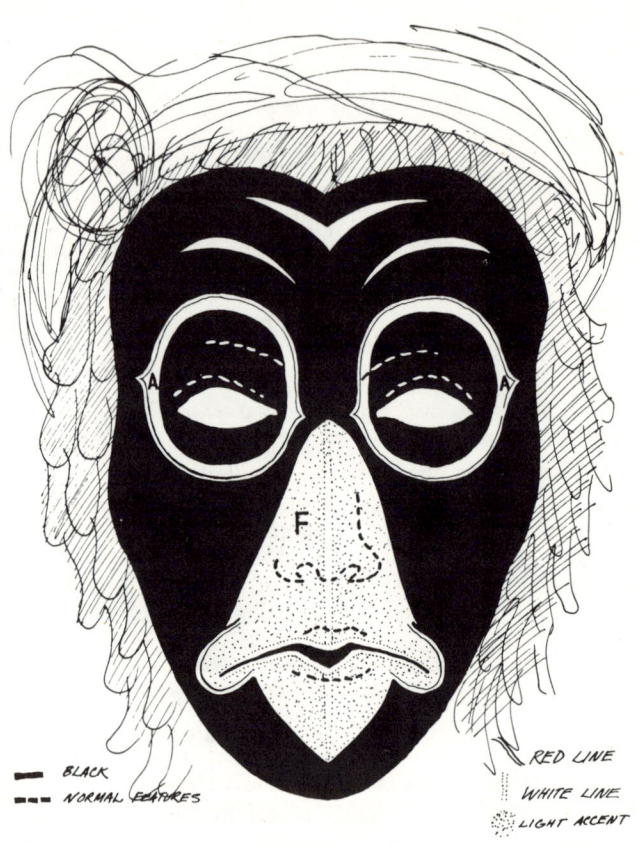

MAKEUP SUPPLIES: *

    Base: #25 Black Base.

    Beak: #16 Yellow Liner.

    Eyes: #22 White Base.

    Accent color: #2 Moist Rouge, medium red.

* *All make-up numbers refer to Stein's grease stick make-up. If other make-up is preferred, please consult their charts to co-relate colours.*

CROW MAKEUP PROCEDURE

1. Draw in all features with #25 Black.
2. Fill in white around the eyes, (Areas A.)
3. Apply Yellow solidly on the beak area, (Area F.)
4. Fill in rest of face solid black. Draw black line of beak over mouth, with the point of the beak being formed on the lower lip.
5. Make thin red lines around the corners of the mouth and around eyes.
6. Draw a white line down the center of the beak, top and bottom.
7. Outline the mouth line in white.

Note: There are no fused lines in this makeup; each area forms a sharp edge against the next one.

REV. EPINARD, THE HEDGEHOG

HEDGEHOG COSTUME PROCEDURE

Materials:
    Leotards and long-sleeved T-Shirt: charcoal grey.
    Mittens: black.
    Socks: black.
    Quills: charcoal grey organdy, white poster paint.
    Padding: one pillow.
    Wimple: charcoal grey broadcloth.
    Robe and Hood: charcoal grey broadcloth, purple trim.

Desired Effect: The crisp points of organdy are very durable, and should serve to give a springy effect to the quills. The padded back and shoulder areas give the proper silhouette to the hedgehog, and at the same time add to the constantly-hovering attention Reverend Epinard gives his Bible. His somewhat somber personality is reflected in the over-all grey effect, with relief coming in the purple decoration on his priestly robe.

1. *Basic Garments:*
   Back padding: Place the pillow behind the back of the actor, with the end protruding above the shoulders, behind the neck. Sew ties just above the shoulders, and two at the waist line. Tie around the waist; cross shoulder strap and tie to opposite waist strap.
   This is worn over the charcoal grey leotards, to which the mittens have been sewed. The socks also could be tacked to the feet of the leotards, to save wear on the leotards.

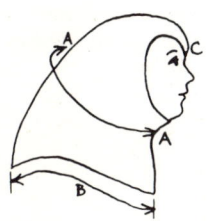

2. *Wimple:*
   Material: Charcoal grey cotton.
   Measurements:
   A. Measure from under the chin around over the pillow to center back.
   B. Measure from center front around shoulders to center back.
   C. Draw extremely low over the forehead, as shown in the makeup sketch.
   Sew as usual, opening under the chin.

3. *Ears:*
   Cut two circles, 6 inches in diameter; one in grey organdy, and one in pink. Make like the ears of the *Lion*. Sew to wimple.

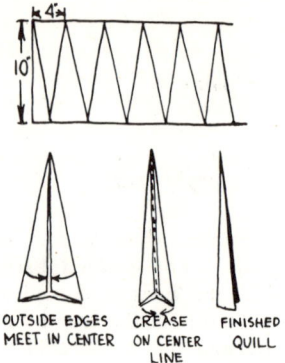

OUTSIDE EDGES MEET IN CENTER   CREASE ON CENTER LINE   FINISHED QUILL

4. *Quills:*

Cut charcoal grey organdy into pieces 12x36 inches. Cut into triangular pieces which measure 4 inches across the bottom.

Crease each side of a triangle to meet in the center. Then crease on the center line. This makes one quill. Dip the tip of each quill 3 inches into a thin mixture of white poster paint, and lay on a newspaper to dry.

Sew quills to the headpiece, laid side by side on the dotted lines. Start at the bottom of the wimple, (line A), and proceed up and around to line B over the forehead. Note that the lines are closer together over the forehead and top of the head. In all cases the seamed edge points upward, and the quill down.

Finally, add one row all the way around the edge of the wimple, (Line C), with spears pointing away from the face.

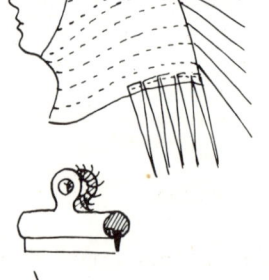

5. *Removable Quills:*

Under one row of quills at the back of the wimple opposite the neck, sew securely in place one strong spring clamp, painted black. Place in this the three "needles" which the Fox pulls out.

6. *Arms and Hands:*

Starting at the knuckle line of the mittens, sew rows of quills, pointing down over the fingers. Continue up the arm, about half way to the elbow.

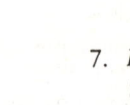

7. *Feet and Legs:*

Starting on top of the toes, sew a row of quills to the foot of the leotards. Continue across the top of the foot and around the ankle, to about mid-calf. The quills may need to be shortened going around the ankle on the sides and back.

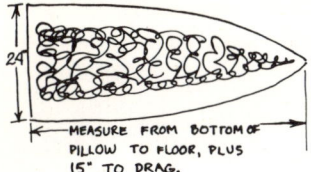

MEASURE FROM BOTTOM OF PILLOW TO FLOOR, PLUS 15" TO DRAG.

8. *Tail:*

   Cut from grey cotton a triangular shaped piece, as shown in the diagram. Cover the outside of the piece with quills, pointing toward the pointed end. Turn wrong side up and place a rounded layer of batting down the center of the triangle. When as round as desired, pull the sides up and over, lapping and whipping in place around the batting. Attach the end of the tail to the lower edge of the pillow.

9. *Robe:*

   Cut from charcoal grey broadcloth.
   Measurements:
   A. Shoulder to floor (in the back measure over the pillow padding).
   B. Neck to wrist.
   C. 15 to 18 inches of sleeve depth.
   D. Waist measurement, (around pillow), plus 6 to 8 inches.

   Sew underarm seams, and finish raw edges. With the robe on the actor, mark with chalk the lines for the purple stripes. This way you can determine how they fall. Cut the stripes from purple brocade, 3 inches wide, (½ inch seams), and sew to robe.

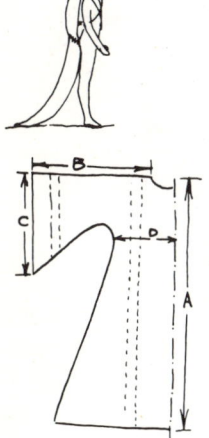

10. *Hood:*

    Material, charcoal grey broadcloth.
    Measurements:
    A. Around the shoulders, plus pillow, plus 6 inches.
    B. Face opening should be 20 to 24 inches (40 to 48 all the way around). It must have room to go around the quills without crushing them.

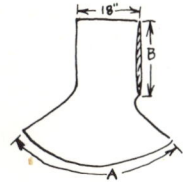

MAKEUP SUPPLIES: *

    Base: #4 Grey Liner.

    Shadow and Lines: #25 Black Base.

    Light Accent Color: #3 Pink Base.

    Teeth: #25 White Base.

* *All make-up numbers refer to Stein's grease stick make-up. If other make-up is preferred, please consult their charts to co-relate colours.*

HEDGEHOG MAKEUP PROCEDURE

1. Apply Grey Liner as base over the entire face.
2. Draw in all lines with Black.
   Fuse the edges of the lines around the cheekbones, chops, chin, sides of nose, and eye bags.
3. Use #3 Pink Base as the light accent color and apply to the following areas:
   Areas A, Above eyes: Accent in the center of the areas above the outside corners of the eyes, fusing edges.
   Areas B, Below eyes: Fill in solidly, fading around the eye, into upper area.
   Area C, Nose: Fill in solidly next to the nose button, and up the bridge of the nose, fading out on the sides.
   Areas D, Chops: Accent in the center, and fade on all sides, leaving a slight trail up the chops and over the cheekbones.
4. Draw in solid black lines all the way around the normal eye, along the sides of the nose to just below the eye, button nose, chops, chin, and whisker dots. In the triangular area left by the chop lines on the upper lip, draw two teeth, shadowing black around them. Shadow black along the headpiece from the eyebrow to the top of the forehead. This color should match the grey of the costume. Lines of the quills could be drawn on the face, corresponding them with those in the headpiece.
5. Fill in teeth with white.

NOBLE, THE LION

LION COSTUME PROCEDURE

Materials:

Cotton mittens.

Long sleeved cotton T-Shirt, and Leotards: yellow-gold.

Men's nylon stretch socks.

Organdy (approximately 6 yards of yellow and gold, 2½ of brown, and 1 of black).

Cotton broadcloth: brown (1 yard).

Several lengths of golden silk organza.

Dacron batting for stuffing tail and feet.

Twill tape.

Brown and gold paint; black ink marker.

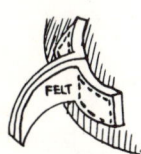

1. *Basic Garments:*

   Buy leotards, with feet, in yellow-gold. Long underwear may be substituted, and dyed to match leotards. Cotton mittens are sewed to the sleeves. Indication of the shape of the paws may be drawn on with a felt tipped ink marker. Claws are cut to a curved shape in a double thickness of black felt. With the ends opened out, sew to the mittens; then saturate claws with thick, cooked starch to stiffen.

   The feet are made by stuffing the end of the sock above the toes with batting. Create the shape of the paw directly on the actor, over the leotard foot. When stuffing is in place, tack the sock to the leotards in several places. Roll the top of the sock down to about 7 inches from the floor. Attach claws the same as they were fastened to the mittens. If long underwear is used, two pairs of socks will be needed, with the first sewed to the bottom of the leg, and the second treated as above.

2. *Wimple:*

   On flat, doubled material, draw out the wimple, using the measurements as shown. It should fit tightly around the face, but should extend comfortably around the neck and down over the shoulders. The opening is at the back of the head, to allow for ease in putting on.

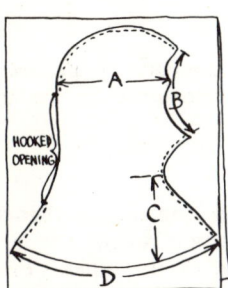

Measurements:

   A. From ½ inch beyond hair line at temple to center back.

   B. From center of forehead around to center under chin, plus 1½ inches.

   C. Allow 8 inches from base of neck out over shoulders.

   D. Measure from center front to center back around top of shoulders, and add 2 inches.

   Sewing: Allow for seams and cut out. Sew together on dotted lines, leaving a 9 inch opening at the back. Fasten opening with hooks and eyes. Stitch elastic under the chin, gathering in extra material to fit around the face. Hem face edge with bias tape.

3. *Ears:*

For ears, cut three circles with a diameter of 12 inches, two in gold organdy, and one in black organdy. Cut them in half. Sew together two semi-circles of gold, and one of black along the straight edge. Turn, leaving gold on one side, and black on the other. Gather along the curved edge drawing it up to measure 3 inches. With black toward front, sew to costume.

4. *Mane:*

Cut yellow and gold organdy in the following sizes, across the width of the fabric.

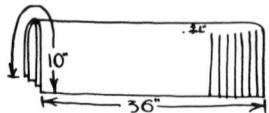

Two 10 inch lengths
Four 16 inch lengths
Three 20 inch lengths
Two 30 inch lengths

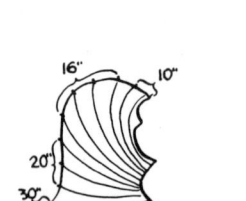

Fold each of these lengths in half, long ways, with the gold doubled on top of the yellow. Cut through the four thicknesses from the raw edge up toward the fold, making strips ½ inch wide. Leave a 1 inch border between the cutting and the folded edge. Do the same for one 40 inch length of brown. Sew folded edge through the four thicknesses, onto the bottom of the wimple. Continue upward, with the longest fringe on the bottom, graduating to the shorter at the top, at about 1½ inch or 2 inch intervals. Cut a special tuft of gold, which finished hangs about 4 inches long, and sew it to the top of the wimple, with sewed ends pointing away from the face, to form the "cowlick". Short tufts, also, would stem from the ears and temples. The entire mane may now be trimmed to create desired shape. The organdy strips will twist and curl, forming the unruly look of the lion's mane. No other material should be substituted. If a heavier mane is preferred, cut more organdy fringe and place at closer intervals.

5. *Elbow Tufts:*

Sew black tufts of organdy, treated as above, on the back of the sleeve, starting about two inches below the elbow, and extending up the arm 6 inches.

6. *Tail:*

Cut two strips of gold organdy 4 inches wide, and long enough that the tail will just clear the floor. Cut two strips of dacron batting the same length, and 1½ inches wide, and lay one on top of the other. Place in the center of the organdy strips, and pull the organdy layers up over the dacron, overlapping in the center. Turn the last edge under, and whip in by hand. Make an organdy tuft of hair out of black, as for the mane. Whip on by hand.

To avoid the usual droop of the costumed tail, it will be necessary to stitch on the inside of the leotards, a 4 inch circle of heavy material, such as canvas ducking, just above the last vertebrae of the actor. To the sides of this attach a belt which may be fastened securely around the hips, hooking in the front. Using twill tape, attach the tail as shown. The tapes will serve to hold the tail away from the body. The tape structure will be covered with a semi-circular piece of organdy.

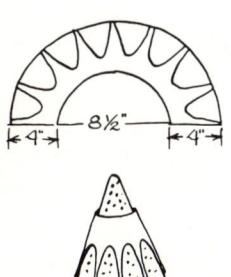

7. *Crown:*

The crown does not fit the head, but perches on top, and must be tacked into place on the wimple. Cut from thick felt, or doubled thin felt. Soak in heavy starch. Shape over a cone shaped object, such as a vegetable ricer, or mixing bowl. Allow to dry. Glue on cotton balls from drapery fringe, or sew on wooden beads. These must be white to simulate pearls. Paint the crown brown, then highlight the edges with gold metallic paint.

8. *Sceptre:*

Make from mitten, stuffed, with thumb basted to the hand section. Delineate toes by lines drawn with inker. Glue on black felt feet pads, using rubber or plastic cement.

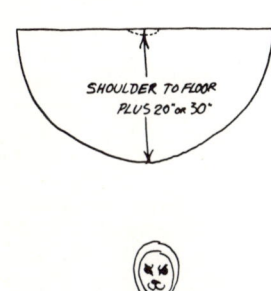

9. *Cape:*

Material: Golden silk organza. This fabric will float behind the king, leaving the tail unhampered. If a heavier fabric is used, such as brocade, it will be necessary to locate a tail exit hole, as for the *Fox.*

Measure the distance from the actor's shoulders to the floor and add 20 to 30 inches for train. The pattern is a plain semi-circle, with a small neck opening cut in the center. Fasten with a band which comes across the shoulders in the front. Several widths of material must be pieced together, depending on the width of the fabric, and height of actor. The cape is worn thrown back over the shoulders.

MAKEUP SUPPLIES: *

    Base: #16 Yellow Liner.

    Shadows: #8 Dark Sunburn Base.

    Light Areas: #22 White Base and a half-and-half mixture of #22 with #16 Yellow Base.

    Eyes, Nose, and Mouth: #25 Black Base.

    Accent Lines: #25 Red-brown Liner.

* All make-up numbers refer to Stein's grease stick make-up. If other make-up is preferred, please consult their charts to co-relate colours.

LION MAKEUP PROCEDURE

1. Apply a small amount of cold cream, and remove with tissues.
2. Apply base: #16 Yellow Liner.
3. Using a brush, and #8 Dark Sunburn Base, draw in all lines, marking off the nose, eyelids, frown puffs, bag below the eyes, chops, chin, cheek bones, temples, and forehead worry lines.
4. Fuse the sides of these lines into the base, so they will not be too harsh. They should still remain dark in the center of the line. Shadow in cheeks and temple areas, from lines back to the edge of the wimple, (Areas L and K). Shadow Area H, under the chops.
5. Apply #22 White Base to the nose, labeled Area A on the chart. This is solid white out to the nose line which has been drawn in, until reaching the area up between the two frown puffs, where it will fade into the base.
6. Apply White to the chops, (Areas B), starting in the center of each, covering solidly next to the mouth and nose, but fading as you reach the outer edges to the right, left, and above.
7. Apply White to the chin, (Area C), with sharp delineation next to the mouth, fading as you approach the chin whiskers.
8. Using Yellow and White, mixed half-and-half, apply to the following areas:

    Areas D, Frown Puffs: Fill in solidly against the frown line, fading out on the open sides.

    Areas E, Upper Eye Puff: Fill in solidly next to the drawn nose and eye lines, fading as you pass over the natural brow into the forehead area.

    Areas F, Lower Eye Puff: Fill in solidly next to lower eye line, fusing into shadow of bag, and fading into cheek bone.

    Area G, Cheek Bones: Make a triangular shape in the center of Area G, and fade out in all directions.

9. Draw in lines with #25 Black Base, around the eyes, nose, mouth, and chops. Lines should be about 1/8 inch thick. The nose is extended beyond the natural nostrils, on each side, and a triangular shape is formed underneath. This line flows into the mouth, or chops line. The chops line starts on the natural mouth, extending past the natural corners, drooping slightly, then rising into a curve. The chin is outlined at the top. Using a small round brush, make the whisker spots. Note that they form two curved lines.

    Pay particular attention to the drawing of the upper eyelid, noticing that the black line swells up in a full curve above the eye, next to the nose, and dips down to the eyelashes before swinging up again. A black "tear" shape is formed below on the inside corner of the eye, and the eye line swells out again toward the outside edge, where it strikes the corner of the eye and swings upward.

10. Using #25 Red-Brown Liner, go back and accent the first lines; in particular, the lines forming the frown, nose, eye bag, chops, chin whiskers, and worry lines in the forehead.

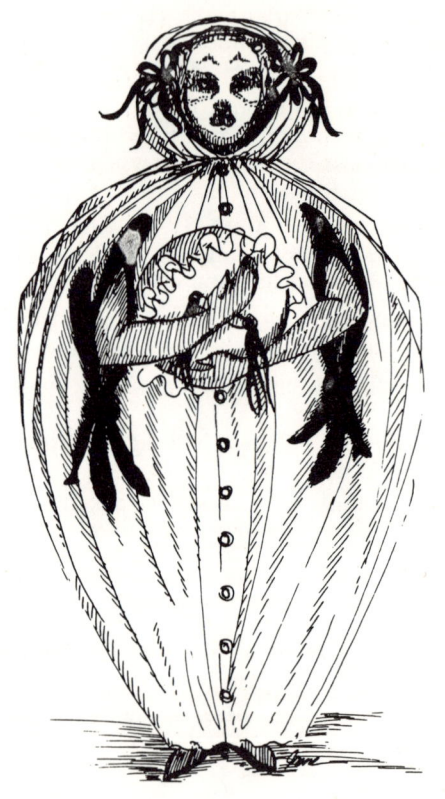

LENDORE, THE MARMOT

MARMOT COSTUME PROCEDURE

Materials:
    Leotards, and long-sleeved T-Shirt: light brown.
    Mittens: light brown.
    Socks: light brown, stretch.
    Wimple: light brown cotton broadcloth.
    Cape: two lengths of net; one gold, one brown.
    Arm-slit trim: pastel orange.
    Pillow: pastel orange (cotton or satin).
    Ribbon: orange satin, 4 yards.
    Brown buttons, 12 plain, round.

Desired Effect: As Mademoiselle Marmot stays in a perpetual state of drowsiness, she can handily withdraw into her cape for a nap. The puffiness of the cape suggests the rotund fluffy quality of the Marmot, and we indulge her femininity to the extent of ribbons on her hood, and her fussy pillow.

1. *Basic Garments:*
The socks are worn over the feet of the leotards, and the mittens are sewed to the sleeves of the T-shirt.

2. *Wimple:*
Cut from light brown cotton; consult directions under *Wolf*.

3. *Ears:*
Cut one circle of light brown, and one of black, with a diameter of 4 inches. Cut circles in half. Sew together a black and brown semicircle, along the curved edge. Turn. Gather across the straight edge. Attach to the wimple, with the black underneath.

4. *Cape:*

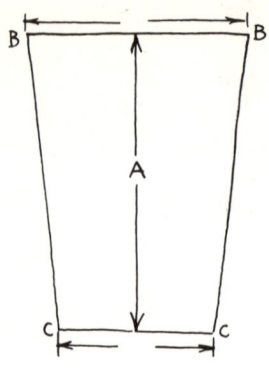

Place the brown and the yellow net together and treat them as one piece of material, with the brown on the outside of the yellow. Fold the material in half, and all four thicknesses may be cut at once.

A. The distance from shoulder to floor plus 6 inches.
B. 72 inches across. This side to be gathered to make the neck.
C. Measure 30 inches, centered.
D. Draw side by connecting lines B and C.

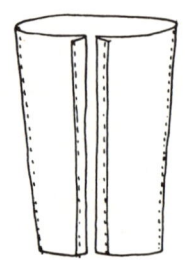

Cut two pieces, from each color, for the front and the back. Split the front section down the center, and sew on two facing strips, 3 inches wide. Stitch the side seams.

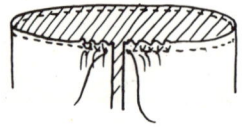

Run a gathering thread along the top edge (line B), and gather to fit loosely around the neck.

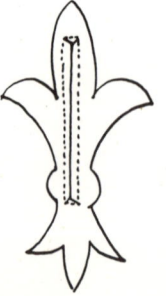

Fit on the actor, and mark slits for the arms, the lower part coming 3 inches below the bottom of the elbow, and extending upward 10 inches Cut *fleur-de-lis* from pastel orange material. Place on the WRONG side of the cape, under the mark for arm-hole. Stitch around the mark, as for a bound buttonhole. Cut between stitching. Pull facing to right side of cape and press flat. Overcast or zig-zag stitch the edges.

To cut the hood, cut a semicircle with a diameter of 36 inches, from both brown and yellow net. Sew straight edges together. Turn. Gather on the curved side to fit neck of cape. Join this gathered edge to fit the gathered neck of the cape.

Because button holes would be too flimsy in net, fasten the front with snaps or hooks and eyes. Sew on brown buttons.

Attach orange satin ribbons to side of hood.

5. *Pillow:*

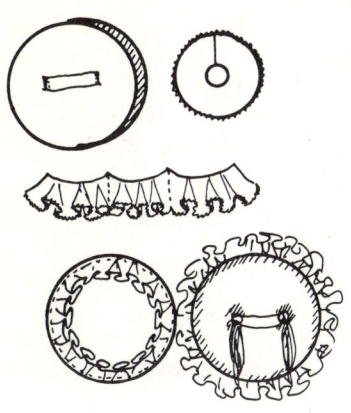

Cut two 16 inch circles of pastel orange material. On one sew a sturdy band of material to be used as a handle. Make ruffles by cutting 9 inch circles with a 2 inch hole in the center. Slit down one side of the circle, and sew several circles together. Pink the outside edge. For fuller effect, double the ruffle. Place the ruffle on the inside edge of one of the pillow circles. Place the other pillow circle on top. Sew all the way around, leaving a few inches through which the pillow may be turned. Stuff with batting, and baste opening. Tack all the way through the pillow at each end of the handle. Attach tassles made from orange ribbons.

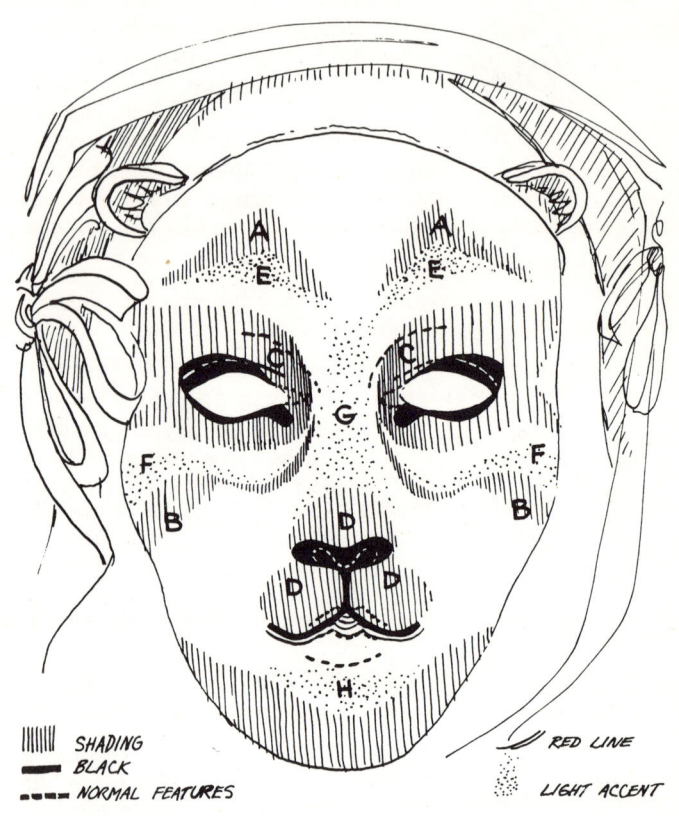

|||| SHADING
— BLACK
---- NORMAL FEATURES
/ RED LINE
: LIGHT ACCENT

MAKEUP SUPPLIES: *

    Base: #7 Brown Liner mixed with #22 White Base.

    Shadow: #7 Brown Liner.

    Light Color Accent: #16 Yellow Liner plus a touch of White.

    Mouth: Moist Rouge #2.

    Lines: #25 Black Base.

* *All make-up numbers refer to Stein's grease stick make-up. If other make-up is preferred, please consult their charts to co-relate colours.*

MARMOT MAKEUP PROCEDURE

1. Apply #7 Brown Liner mixed with #22 White Base to entire face. This color should match the color of the wimple.

2. Using #7 Brown Liner, draw in all lines and areas, including the shape of the eyes, the areas around the eyes, pouches in the forehead, cheek lines, dark areas around the nose and chops, mouth line, and the chin.

3. Using #7 Brown Liner as the shadow color:
   Areas A: Shade the areas above the pouches in the forehead, making it darker next to the pouch line, and fading into the base color above.
   Areas B: Brush in shadow color under the cheek lines, fading out as you go down.
   Areas C: Fill in the shape around the eyes. Then add a touch of #25 Black Base to the brown, and darken the areas next to the nose, fading out as you reach the center of the eyes.
   Area D: Fill in the nose and chop area with #7 Brown Liner.

4. Using #25 Black Base:
   Paint in solid the black eye, in the shape shown.
   Begin the black nose at the tip of the actor's nose, and continue under the nostrils.
   Begin the black mouth line under the nose, going down to the top of the lip, then swing down under the top lip and slightly up at the corners of the mouth.

5. Apply red #2 Moist Rouge under the black mouth line, filling in the small triangle formed at the center of the top lip.

6. Mix #16 Yellow Liner with just a touch of #7 Brown Liner to make the light accent color. If a stronger contrast is needed with the base, add white, also. Apply as follows:
   Areas E: Accent pouches above the eyes, heavily next to the shadow, fading on the under side.
   Areas F: Accent the cheek bones, trailing off to a narrow area as you approach the eyes.
   Areas G: Accent the bridge of the nose, fusing edges, and stopping when you reach the dark nose area (D).
   Area H: Accent center of chin, fading edges.

The Corey costume-make-up designs were planned to make the human actor resemble his animal character as nearly as possible. Working from an entirely different concept, another distinguished costume artist, Miss Lucy Barton, of the University of Texas, created costumes for this play deliberately calculated to portray the animal character in human terms. Her notes, therefore, reflect a radically different approach to the over-all costume plan.

ALTERNATIVE COSTUME SUGGESTIONS
by Lucy Barton

In costuming any play with animal characters, the first question to be answered is — "Are the actors to be men disguised as animals, or men suggesting the idea of animals?" In the Texas production of REYNARD THE FOX, it was decided that the costumer's aim should be suggestion, rather than imitation. Here, it was agreed, are men with traits that tradition has assigned to various animals. The costumer's task, therefore, was to find a visual statement for each animal-man, and express it clearly for an audience of children or adults.

In any production, the first impression on an audience is made by colour. Hence, in costuming REYNARD THE FOX, colour was used freely to express character. Moreover, because this is a play for children, who delight in colour, the protective colouration of the real animals was generally ignored, in favour of strong, bright hues, assuring a stage full of gaiety. The bright garments were fitted to human bodies. Additional touches proclaimed the animal character of each.

TIECELIN THE CROW, a sleek, vain bird, wore a slim tunic and tights of silk, iridescent in blue-green-black. The tunic was edged to hip length with feather-shaped pieces of the silk. The same sort of feathers, sewed in overlapping layers on a drapery extending from wrist to wrist and attached to the back, formed wings. His close-fitting cap had a projecting yellow visor like a beak. His tail, made of buckram reinforced with milliner's wire, was covered with layers of the feathers, three of which could be pulled away.

EPINARD THE HEDGEHOG, wearing the conventional clerical black with a white neck-cloth known as "geneva bands", was distinguished by a close cap bristling with quills which extended also in a long queue hanging halfway down his back. (The quills were pipe-cleaners, dyed black).

BRUN THE BEAR expressed his bearish quality by his clumsy, bulky garments. All of him, including hands and feet, was covered in dark blue corduroy made up over a complete quilted padding. His close cap with small pink-lined ears was made (over padding) of dark brown fur-fabric. This fur continued in a strip down his back and on to form a wide, thick tail.

YSENGRIN THE WOLF, a great contrast to Bear, was lithe and sleek in dark blue-green silk. His cap, spinal strip and long tail were fashioned from gray fur fabric the color of a timber wolf. His ears stood up smartly because the white silk lining was wired. When one of them was pulled away, that ear flopped dejectedly.

NOBLE THE LION was primarily a king-figure in purple velvet tunic and silk tights, nearly covered by a royal robe of crimson velvet with ermine cape. He had a gold chain and a leopard-skin tabbed belt encrusted with gold. His small but glittering crown sat very slightly askew on his huge leonine wig (made of ravelled new hemp rope).

REYNARD THE FOX, in contrast to his principal antagonist the green-clad wolf, wore bright orange-red tunic and tights. His sleek cap, spinal strip and expressive tail were made of fur-fabric like the pelt of the red fox. His pointed ears stood up pertly.

LENDORE THE MARMOT bore little resemblance to the real animal except for her roundness. She wore a padded dress that made her soft and shapeless and comfortable-looking. Even her head and feet were padded, the outer layer being gold-colored corduroy. She carried a soft round pillow of a slightly darker color.

MAKE-UP

All the animals were made up to emphasize their characters, but the make-up was in no sense an animal mask. The emphasis was often achieved by eye-brows, beards and moustaches like the animal fur of the caps. A piece of Bear's moustache came off, to conform to the business required. Lendore was just pretty, like a motherly young woman. The fox's eyebrows were pointed, and his moustache and beard were small and neat. Lion's beard was like his hair. Epinard was not bearded, nor was Tiecelin.